ON CALL

ON CALL

A Rural Surgeon's Story

J. LOTTMANN, MD

ON CALL
A RURAL SURGEON'S STORY

Copyright © 2014 J. LOTTMANN, MD.

All rights reserved. No part of this book may be used or reproduced by any means, graphic, electronic, or mechanical, including photocopying, recording, taping or by any information storage retrieval system without the written permission of the publisher except in the case of brief quotations embodied in critical articles and reviews.

iUniverse books may be ordered through booksellers or by contacting:

iUniverse
1663 Liberty Drive
Bloomington, IN 47403
www.iuniverse.com
1-800-Authors (1-800-288-4677)

Because of the dynamic nature of the Internet, any web addresses or links contained in this book may have changed since publication and may no longer be valid. The views expressed in this work are solely those of the author and do not necessarily reflect the views of the publisher, and the publisher hereby disclaims any responsibility for them.

Any people depicted in stock imagery provided by Thinkstock are models, and such images are being used for illustrative purposes only. Certain stock imagery © Thinkstock.

ISBN: 978-1-4917-4515-1 (sc)
ISBN: 978-1-4917-4514-4 (e)

Library of Congress Control Number: 2014917454

Printed in the United States of America.

iUniverse rev. date: 10/24/2014

Contents

Introduction vii

1	The Making of a Surgeon	1
2	Medical School	6
3	Internship	17
4	Residency	22
5	Chief Resident	41
6	My First Job	46
7	Sparta, Wisconsin	49
8	Credentials and Teaching	56
9	Clinic Business	61
10	Marriage and Motherhood	66
11	Faith	74
12	1993	79
13	Hospital Politics	89
14	Lawsuits	102
15	Interesting Cases—Obstetrics	116
16	Trauma	125
17	Interesting Cases—General Surgery	130
18	The Least Expensive Carpal Tunnel Release	145
19	On Call	149
20	Being a Rural Surgeon	156
21	Being a Female Surgeon	169
22	Completing My Call	172

Introduction

This is the story of a female rural surgeon. There aren't very many of us around, so mine is an uncommon story. It spans a thirty-year practice (1981–2011) after schooling and training. My intent is to show the distinctiveness of a rural surgery practice and how it differs from an urban practice. I will also share how the scope of general surgery and my particular surgical caseload changed over that thirty-year period. This story includes the challenges of being a wife and mother as well as being a surgeon—frequently, the only surgeon in town.

The call came at about 2:30 a.m. It woke me from a sound sleep. The caller said, "This is Tomah Hospital. We need you for a stat C-section."

I said, "Okay. I'll be right there."

I got up, quickly put on a shirt and pants, slipped on my sandals, and headed out the door.

I live about a quarter mile from Interstate 90. I took the freeway for a short distance and exited to Highway 16. That would bring me closer to the hospital when I got to Tomah, which was about fifteen minutes away.

I could call the hospital on my way to learn more about the situation, but my primary intent was to get there as fast as I could because either the mother or the baby or both were in distress. On the way, I mentally reviewed what would need to be done.

When I got to the hospital, I went directly to the locker room, quickly changed clothes, and went into the OR. The OB provider met me in the OR and filled me in on the details.

The patient was a thirty-one-year-old Amish woman. This was her seventh pregnancy. She had had a stillborn with her last pregnancy. All her previous babies had been delivered by the Amish lay midwife. She was in active labor. She had started bleeding heavily with each contraction, so they brought her to the hospital. She had soaked three or four folded blankets with blood at home. She had had no prenatal care.

An ultrasound at the hospital had revealed that she had a placenta previa. The placenta was at the bottom of the uterus, over the outlet, and as the cervix dilated, the placenta was separating from the uterus and bleeding. As the placenta pulled away, less oxygen was getting to the baby. The only way to stop the bleeding and save the baby was to do a C-section.

As the OB provider was telling me this, I was helping hold the patient in the proper position so the anesthetist could place the spinal anesthetic.

Once the spinal was in, we scrubbed and gowned up as the nurse prepped the patient. Another physician was present to care for the baby. We draped the patient, and I asked my assisting physician to put his finger on the patient's left iliac crest while I put my finger on the right one to orient me to the anatomy.

Anesthesia gave me the go ahead, so I made the skin incision—a slightly curved horizontal incision in the lower abdomen—from just shy of one iliac crest to just shy of the other.

I extended the incision through the fat and down to the muscle fascia. Then I cut across that fascia. Lifting the upper cut edge with clamps, I pushed the muscle away on both sides and then cut up the midline to just below the belly button. I did the same thing by lifting the lower edge of the fascia and cutting down to the pubic bone. I divided the muscle at the midline and tented the peritoneum between clamps. When I cut the peritoneum, I was in the abdomen.

I then pushed the large uterus up toward the patient's head and made a small incision where the peritoneum reflected onto the bladder. I pushed the bladder down to get it away from where I was going to make my incision in the uterus. I made a small horizontal incision in the uterus. I extended the incision with my fingers in both directions. The first thing I encountered was the placenta, but it pushed away easily. I then saw the amniotic sac. I opened it with care so as not to injure the baby. The waters had already broken, so there wasn't much separating me from the baby. I found the baby's legs, but there appeared to be a narrowing of the uterus that wasn't allowing the rest of the baby to come down. With my assistant putting pressure on the uterus from above and me gently pulling on the legs, we were able to deliver the baby. The cord was clamped, and the baby was handed off to the physician who was there to care for the baby. The baby looked good.

The placenta wasn't attached to much anymore, so it came out easily. All was well.

I closed the uterus with two rows of sutures.

Below the closed uterine incision, there was a bleeder near the bladder that was bleeding more than I wanted to leave behind. I put in a figure eight suture around it to stop the bleeding. Once I tied the suture, I had what looked like four fountains of bleeding instead of one bleeder, one at each hole where the needle went in the tissue. This was the area where the placenta had been attached, and it was apparently very thin and tenuous.

I put pressure on the spot for five minutes. Pressure stopped the bleeding, but when I let up on the pressure, it started bleeding again. I didn't think putting in more sutures would help. I tried a fibrinolytic agent that was supposed to help stop bleeding, but after putting on the agent and putting on pressure for another five minutes, it didn't stop or even slow down. I had control of the bleeding when I had pressure on the area, but I couldn't close the patient with my hand in there.

I tried more of the fibrinolytic agent and more pressure, but nothing seemed to help. She was bleeding more.

I told the anesthetist he needed to put the patient to sleep. The spinal anesthetic we used only lasts about an hour, and she was starting to feel things. Further, with her previous blood loss and what we were currently losing, we needed to start thinking about giving her some blood replacement.

I considered my options. We could attempt to control the blood that was coming to the area by tying off the two large arteries that supply the uterus, but doing that would not guarantee that we would control the bleeding. An area so low on the uterus may have blood supply from the vagina as well. If we removed the uterus, in other words, did a hysterectomy, we would stop the bleeding because we would be removing the part that was bleeding. I decided to do a hysterectomy.

I asked the nurse to call the other surgeon who was in the area to see if he could come in to help. Thankfully, he was available and came in.

We would soon use up all the blood products we had available at the hospital that were compatible with this patient. We called in the maintenance personnel and sent them to La Crosse to get more. We called ahead to order what we thought we would need. They made more than one trip that early morning.

With the help of the other surgeon, I was able to do the hysterectomy. Everything seemed to bleed. A pregnant uterus is very vascular. We finally were to the point where the uterus was out and the vagina was closed. There were a couple of bleeders at the corners of the vaginal cuff that stopped with further suturing. There was still a little oozing in the pelvis, but no specific bleeder, and I thought by closing the abdomen we would be creating enough intra-abdominal pressure on the area to control it.

We closed the abdomen, put on the dressing, and took the patient to the recovery room. She was stable but very pale. We had given her four units of blood and some platelets and fresh frozen plasma to replace her clotting factors. I estimated we had lost about ten units of blood. The circulating nurse told me she couldn't lift the bag of bloody sponges when we were done.

We finished the case at about 6 a.m. I dictated my operative note and rested for a while. I had surgical cases scheduled in the OR at 8 a.m.

I finished my surgical cases at about 11:30 a.m. and then went to the special care unit to see how the patient was doing. She looked so pale that I actually thought she could be dead. I stood at her beside and watched to see if she was breathing. She was. Her blood count was seven point nine (normal is eleven). The nurse said her blood pressure was hovering around ninety, which was low for her. I told the nurse to give her all the blood products we had left.

I then went to Sparta to prepare for my afternoon clinic. I started seeing patients at 1 p.m. At about 1:30, the special care unit nurse in Tomah called to tell me that the patient was awake, sitting up in bed, and nursing the baby. Her blood pressure was normal, and her blood count was improved. Thank you, God!

After supper that night, I had my husband drive me back to Tomah to see the patient. I was too tired to drive safely. I didn't think I could sleep unless I saw her again because the last time I had seen her she looked so bad. She now looked good, and I got a good night's sleep.

The next day, I reflected on how I had gotten to the point where I was doing this kind of surgery on this kind of patient in the middle of the night with limited resources. This book is my story. I take you through my training, my practice, some of my most memorable cases, my triumphs, and some of my challenges. I also share my life as a wife and mother. I am hopeful that my story will encourage students to pursue a career in rural surgery.

1

The Making of a Surgeon

I was raised on a dairy farm in Minnesota. When I called my parents to tell them I had decided to go into surgery, my mother's response was, "I could have told you that." She said she knew because I was always in the thick of the butchering process on the farm and had shown an interest in how the animals were put together. We had chickens and pigs as well as cows, and we did all our own butchering. My older sister (by twenty-two months) worked with Mom in the house, and I worked outside with Dad. I liked to dress like him in coveralls and cap. I was a tomboy through and through.

We didn't have much money. We lived in the house my mom had been raised in. We didn't have an indoor bathroom until I was twelve, and we didn't have television until I was in eighth grade. Mom sewed our clothes (pajamas out of feed sacks), or we wore hand-me-downs. I was in seventh grade when I got my first store-bought dress. That was a big deal!

I enjoyed school, and I always did well. I liked math and science, and in high school I was the only girl in the trigonometry and physics classes. My dad quit farming and became a life-insurance salesman when I was in middle school. We continued to live on the farm and rented out the land. We retained one milk cow, and it was my responsibility to milk her morning and evening, by hand. We made our own butter from the cream. Her calf became my pet.

I read a lot, nearly all the books in the school library, but I didn't pay attention to specific word meanings. I always assumed their meaning from the context. I graduated high school valedictorian of the class despite getting a D on my vocabulary test in English my senior year. My birthday is December 29, so I was the youngest person in the class and was voted the most likely to succeed in science.

The day after I graduated from high school, my family moved from the farm to a home on a lake in north-central Minnesota. I helped Mom get settled. I like to organize things, so I put away most of the stuff in the new house. During my first semester at college, it wasn't uncommon for Mom to call me to ask where something was. I could usually tell her.

It was assumed I would go to college. I followed my older sister to Augustana College in Sioux Falls, South Dakota. I enrolled in math and science classes because that was what I liked. That was considered a premed program. I did well in college without much effort. I watched a lot of television, trying to catch up on all the programs I had missed as a kid. I was in the marching band, continued to read a lot, worked as a lab assistant, went to a lot of movies, listened to music, and did a little bit of studying. I double majored in biology and chemistry and minored in math.

The summer between my junior and senior year, I stayed on campus and did biochemistry research. I eventually published a paper titled, "The Carbon Dioxide Fixation Cycle in Acanthamoeba Castellanii." We used a computer to analyze the data. The computer took up an entire room that was temperature controlled, and you programmed the computer by typing input cards, one line of code per card. If you missed a period, the program wouldn't run. That could be exasperating!

Biochemistry was the first class that challenged me. Everyone in the class failed the first test. I had to knuckle down and study.

In developmental biology my senior year, we did an experiment on chick embryos to try to create spina bifida, a condition where the bone, muscle, and skin fail to close over the spinal cord in the lower back. When the chick embryo was seventy-two hours old, we cut a little window in the eggshell and, with a tungsten needle under binoculars, attempted to disrupt the notochord—the precursor of the spinal cord and structures over it. Then we put a piece of tape over the hole in the shell and put the egg back into the incubator to mature and hatch. My chick was the only one that hatched with the desired defect. Later the instructor told me that everyone who had had a successful outcome with this experiment in the previous ten years had become a surgeon.

In thinking about what I was going to do after college, I knew I wanted to continue going to school, so I took the MCAT exam for medical school and the GRE exam in chemistry for graduate school. I did better on the MCAT exam, earning very high scores in math and science, (my English score was lower than that of a friend of mine who was from China) so I looked into going to medical school.

I didn't know anything about being a doctor. We rarely had a need to seek medical care. Mom usually took care of our medical needs. She once removed a metal sliver from my eyelid with a razor blade and dressed my big toe when I nearly cut it off on a can lid when I had jumped into the lake. I didn't know any doctors personally, and I had never worked in a hospital or clinic. I had been a patient several times, however. I'd had a broken forearm as a kid that took seven attempts to set. I'd had my appendix out in junior high, and I'd had a very bad sinus infection that required two weeks of hospitalization on IV antibiotics the summer after I graduated high school. But I never paid any attention to what the doctor did.

My advisor in college was the biochemistry teacher with whom I had done research, and he advised me to apply to med schools that were research oriented. I applied to the University of Minnesota, the University of Chicago Pritzker School of Medicine, and Baylor University in Texas. I was eventually accepted at all three but decided

I didn't want to leave the Midwest. I heard from the University of Minnesota right away that I had been assigned a room in a fraternity. That didn't sound right.

A good friend of mine was accepted at the University of Chicago. We had done research together, and we had taken all the same classes at Augustana with all the same grades. I decided I wanted to go to the University of Chicago, too, and applied. I didn't hear from the school for a long time. I was beginning to think I wasn't being accepted because I was female. That was the only difference between my friend and me. We were even both interviewed for the University of Chicago by the same surgeon alumnus, Dr. Savage, who lived in Yankton, South Dakota.

I finally called the registration office at the University of Chicago and pressed them for a response. Initially they couldn't find my application. Then they called and apologized and said they had found it behind a file cabinet. They said they would put me down as the first name on the alternate list because the class was full. Someone must have decided not to go to the University of Chicago Pritzker School of Medicine, because I soon got a call that I had been accepted. I was in.

Graduating from college was almost anticlimactic. I graduated summa cum laude with a 4.0 grade point average. I couldn't wait to see what medical school would be like.

I have to tell you about the car I had my last year of college. "Old Blue" was a 1962 Ford Falcon. I bought it for two hundred dollars. It was white, but I painted it International-Harvester blue using a paintbrush. The floorboard under the driver's seat was rusted away and had been replaced with a Coke sign. It could get very cold driving in the winter, and I needed a blanket on my left leg to keep it warm. One holiday I was going to drive home, but the car wouldn't start. I borrowed a galvanometer from the physics department and tested the wiring to see if there was current where it was supposed to be. I determined that it was the starter that was faulty, so I got someone to give me a push to get it started and drove home the eight hours it took without turning the car off. My dad and I replaced the brushes in the starter for five dollars, and it worked fine the rest of the time I had it. I sold the car for two hundred dollars before I went to medical school.

2
Medical School

The first event of medical school was a wine-and-cheese party hosted by the dean of the medical school. During the party, Dean Ceithamel walked right up to me and said, "You must be Judy Lottmann. Tell me, how does your mother can mushrooms?"

On the back page of the application form for medical school, there was a place for a passport-sized photo and a large blank area for you to tell something about yourself. I couldn't think of anything to write about myself, so I wrote about what I was doing. I was home for the summer helping Mom garden and can produce. I wrote about how we had canned 110 quarts of string beans and 50 quarts of peaches.

So, that was where the dean had heard about my mother's canning. I had to respond to his question by telling him that my mother didn't can mushrooms, but after that day the dean knew who I was, and whenever a grant or scholarship opportunity crossed his desk that he thought I might qualify for, he would call me in to fill out an application. I had very limited financial resources, so he helped me out a lot. Of course, his knowing who I was also meant that if he needed a freshman representative on a committee, he frequently asked me to participate. In retrospect, that helped me learn about leadership and how committees work.

The first two years of medical school were like college classes, but they were more of a challenge. All my classmates were from the top 5 percent of their college classes. The professors did research and during class talked about what they were working on. We were responsible to learn what was in the textbooks ourselves. Luckily it was a pass/fail system. I did okay once I figured out how it all worked.

I remember one class in physiology when we were studying how the heart muscle worked. A student asked the professor if he knew why the muscle did what he had just told us. The professor said yes. He wouldn't tell us any more information because he hadn't published his findings yet.

One of our first classes was anatomy. I loved it. We dissected a cadaver. We named our cadaver "Earnest" so we could say we were working in "dead earnest." We worked in groups of four students per cadaver. I was in a group that included my friend from college, Gene, the token student from South Dakota; Pat, the token student from Montana; and a young man from Chicago. Most everyone else was from the East or West Coast or from Chicago. I was the token student from Minnesota.

I don't think the young man from Chicago had ever been outside the city limits. By the end of the anatomy class, Gene, Pat, and I had convinced him that we still lived in the horse-and-buggy days in Minnesota, South Dakota, and Montana. Convincing him of this was possible because at least one student in the class thought South Dakota was a suburb of Minneapolis!

At times, I felt like a foreign student. Not many were from a farm or rural area. One of my classmates actually told me, "I'm surprised that you are proud of where you come from."

My uncle had given me a pair of cowboy boots as I left for medical school. I had never worn cowboy boots before, but they served me well in Chicago. If I wore them with my jeans and parka, you couldn't tell if I was a male or female walking down the street. This was an advantage, because the streets weren't safe for a woman.

I lived in a dorm that was an old hotel that had previously been owned by the Mafia. It was directly in front of the Museum of Science and Industry and about a mile from the University of Chicago campus. I walked to and from class every day. We were told to carry a whistle and have at least twenty-five dollars in our pockets at all times. If you were held up, you could blow the whistle, and if that didn't scare the thief away, maybe twenty-five dollars would satisfy him so he wouldn't hurt you. I never had a whistle, and I never carried twenty-five dollars. Since I was on a very strict budget—loans, grants, and scholarships—I couldn't afford to lose twenty-five dollars.

The year I started medical school was the first year they had women in the dorm I lived in. There were very few of us. I remember watching television one night (yes, I did that in medical school, too) when I was the only girl in the room. We were watching *The Autobiography of Miss Jane Pitman*. Suddenly a commercial came on for sanitary napkins—the first such ad I had ever seen. I was so embarrassed that I slunk down in my chair as far as I could go. That was quite a traumatic experience for me.

My mother had taught all her daughters how to sew, and even into medical school I sewed my own clothes. The only place in the dorm with a surface big enough to lay out the fabric was the ping-pong table. My fellow residents did not appreciate it when I tied up the table for the whole evening cutting out a pattern.

I had no refrigerator in my dorm room, nor did I have access to one. During the winter, I would use the windowsill as my refrigerator. I kept half a dozen eggs, milk, and bread outside on the windowsill. When my bread got stale, I would make bread pudding in the microwave in the student lounge. Back then, you couldn't program the microwave. It had pre-set times. I learned that it took me seven times on the sandwich setting to get my bread pudding done. I also learned to make toast on the hotplate of a popcorn popper. I would lay my piece of bread on a pair of pliers laid over the hotplate. It didn't take very long. Eventually I graduated to an electric frying pan.

I didn't have a car when I was in medical school. I traveled to and from medical school on the Amtrak train from Minneapolis. The train station in Chicago was in the basement of the Sears Tower. If I arrived at the end of the work day, I couldn't walk toward the lake to catch my local train because the sidewalk traffic was so thick going in the other direction. I would have to wait until the foot traffic thinned out a little. It surprised me that there were so many people in downtown Chicago.

I spent six weeks of the summer between my first and second years of medical school at the Gallup Indian Medical Center in Gallup, New Mexico. Three other students from the University of Chicago and two students from Yale were there as well. We four students from the University of Chicago rented an unfurnished apartment and slept on the floor in sleeping bags. I even had to borrow the sleeping bag, as I had no money to buy one. I was assigned to do a rotation on obstetrics and gynecology. While we were there, the clinic held its annual pap and pelvic day for the women from the Navajo reservation. They set me up in an exam room and showed me what to do. I was to have someone come and look if I found anything out of the ordinary. Some of the Native American women I examined didn't wear any underwear and simply lifted their skirts to get on the exam table. I was told the smell was from the fact that they voided standing in place and then trapped the odor under their long skirts.

The one baby I recall delivering was a woman's twelfth child, and she came in ready to deliver. There was no time for any prep. With, I think, her first push, the baby came out, along with a lot of feces and urine. I was covered in it. I decided then and there that I didn't want to do obstetrics.

The doctors in Gallup encouraged us to see the sights while we were there, so every weekend we ventured out. We visited Canyon

De Chelly National Monument, the Havasupai Indian Village, Havasupai Falls, Chaco Canyon, Window Rock, and Santa Fe, and one weekend we slept in a hogan and cooked outside like the Navajos. A hogan is the traditional dwelling of the Navajo. It is a rounded hut set over a dug-out area that is about two steps down when you enter. There was a small wood stove inside for heat in the winter. When we went in, we discovered a round snake coiled around the stovepipe. We removed him before we settled in for the night. He was there again when we woke in the morning. We couldn't figure out how he got there without going over one of us.

In the fall of my second year of medical school, my older sister got married, and I was in the wedding. I flew home for the weekend. I didn't take many clothes because I wasn't going to be home long, and my family had my bridesmaid's dress already. Since I had the extra space, I decided to fill my suitcase with potatoes, apples, carrots, cabbage, squash, and other produce for my return trip to Chicago. We were late getting to the airport, so I couldn't check my luggage. I had to take it through the inspection line. Imagine the surprise on the inspectors' faces when they opened my suitcase! They did let me get on the plane.

During the third year of medical school, students rotate through various medical specialties. I eliminated them as I went. I didn't like pediatrics because I didn't like dealing with sick kids. In psychiatry, I was very easily manipulated by the patients. On one internal medicine rotation, we saw only ulcerative colitis patients because that was the disease the attending doctor was studying. On neurology, I remember seeing a patient who had been a boxing champion and who could now hardly lift his head. He had myasthenia gravis, a relatively rare disease that is sometimes associated with a tumor of the thymus. On dermatology, everyone walked around in plastic wrap because of severe dermatitis. We also saw multiple patients with mycosis fungoides, a rare skin disease. I haven't seen a case since.

My rotation on obstetrics and gynecology was very traumatic. I witnessed the delivery of the baby of a very large lady who was a prostitute. She refused to push when it was time to birth her baby. The nurses had to push on her abdomen to get the baby out. Later I was in attendance for a delivery of a fourteen-year-old who didn't know where the baby was going to come out and had to have a procedure before she could deliver because she had a thick vaginal septum. This reinforced my decision not to do obstetrics. I also witnessed a procedure to trim the labia majora of a prostitute so she would "look better," and I scrubbed in for a procedure to create a vagina for a young lady who was born without one. That was not a routine experience. I don't recall if I ever saw a hysterectomy. Luckily, I came down with infectious mononucleosis on this rotation and had to go home to recuperate because my spleen got very large. They credited my time in Gallup so I wouldn't have to repeat the rotation.

As a medical student rotating on a service, I took the patient's history and did a physical exam. I wrote up my findings and presented them to the medical team on rounds. The only comment I got on my write-ups was that they sounded like letters home.

Surgery was my last rotation, and I felt as if I had come home. I got to do a lot as a medical student because the intern and senior resident on the service were out sick with hepatitis. They had contracted the disease when tying wire sutures to close the sternum of a heart-surgery patient who'd had hepatitis. It was just the junior resident and two medical students caring for all the patients on the service. I don't know how much of an influence this had on me, but I knew I loved it. It didn't seem like I made a decision to go into surgery; it was simply where I belonged.

I thought I wanted to practice in a small community (since I knew that was where I wanted to live), so the summer between my third and fourth year of medical school I looked for an opportunity to spend some time in such a setting and see what that would be like.

Two of the surgeons on staff at the University of Chicago Hospital had been tent mates in a MASH unit with Dr. C. B. McVay during the Korean War. Dr. McVay practiced in Yankton, South Dakota. Arrangements were made for me to do a surgical rotation for a month in Yankton. Dr. McVay is known for a repair he developed for inguinal hernias. The local surgeons got a good laugh when they assigned me to work up a patient who was a farmer and had a very large inguinal hernia. The patient didn't want to take his long underwear off for the exam.

I also spent a month working with (following around) the family practice doctors in the town where my folks lived. On one occasion, I got to ride in the ambulance with a stroke patient being transferred to a Duluth hospital. It was a very good experience and confirmed my decision to work in a small community.

Since I was planning on going into general surgery, I elected to rotate through other specialties my senior year, ones I wouldn't have an opportunity to do otherwise. I did a rotation on plastic surgery because I wanted to know how to close wounds with the least scarring. I did endocrinology because it is closely related to endocrine surgery. I did infectious diseases, pharmacology, anesthesiology, and radiology because they are all related fields I would use in surgery. I also taught in the anatomy lab and took the course "Readings in General Internal Medicine" to round out my medical education.

Once a medical student has decided what specialty to go into, the fall of senior year is spent interviewing for a residency-training program. Each year a book is published that lists all the residency programs in the United States and surrounding countries. A medical student chooses which ones are of interest and arranges to go for an interview. I decided to look into the surgery residency programs at Hennepin County Hospital in Minneapolis, Minnesota; St. Paul Ramsey Hospital in St. Paul, Minnesota; the hospital in Yankton, South Dakota; the University of Vermont in Burlington, Vermont; and the University of North Carolina in Chapel Hill, North Carolina. I wanted a relatively small program that was oriented to rural practice. I had no interest in staying at the University of Chicago. The chairman of the department of surgery, Dr. Skinner, even though he was interested in me as a candidate for residency, agreed that staying in Chicago would not be in my best interest.

Living in Chicago had been a bit traumatic for me. During my four years in Chicago, I was robbed twice. The first time the thief grabbed my clutch purse from the top of my pile of books. I didn't have much money in the purse, but I lost my driver's license and ID. I spent the night in the police station waiting for the police to capture the thief so I could identify him. The second time, the thief entered my apartment and stole my books, the only things I had of value. In the process, he ransacked the entire apartment, and I didn't feel safe there anymore. I finished my senior year living in the hospital residents' housing.

I was the only one of the twenty-five women in my medical school class of one hundred students who went into surgery.

So off I went to interview. When I went to Burlington, Vermont, I flew in at night. I knew nothing about the area and had no idea where my motel was. It was a small airport, and there were taxis waiting at the front door. I told one of the drivers where I needed to go and got in the car. He drove about a block down the street, and there was my motel. Okay! I checked in and went to bed. When I got up in the morning, I pulled the curtain open to see what it looked like: all I could see were woods, no buildings. Where was I? As it turned out, Burlington was a quaint little New England town with the church steeple and all. My interview went well. It was a good program.

When I went for my interview at Chapel Hill, North Carolina, it had snowed a couple of inches during the night. I found out that airports in that area didn't have much equipment to clear snow and ice from the runways. I remember the plane approaching the runway, but when we got to about treetop level, the pilot informed us that we couldn't land there and would have to go to Greensboro. So we gained altitude and flew a few minutes and then started to descend. Again, once we got to about treetop level, the pilot said no, we couldn't land and would have to go back to Chapel Hill. We eventually landed at Chapel Hill, but every time the pilot applied the brakes, the plane would start sliding to one side or the other. Finally we stopped. Thank goodness for long runways.

When I arrived at the surgery department in the hospital, the chairman wasn't in his office, but they told me to take a seat and he would be in shortly. When he came in, he patted me on the head as he walked by and said, "So you're a little girl who wants to go into surgery." I decided that that program wasn't for me.

I remember interviewing for Hennepin County's program with Dr. Sutherland. His first question for me was, "So, you're smart! What else have you got to offer?" I don't remember how I responded. I was not favorably impressed.

I decided against Yankton, South Dakota, because although it was a good program, it seemed to me that everyone there had been taught by Dr. McVay and did everything the same. I wanted a variety of teachers so I could choose what worked best for me.

I don't remember much about my interview at St. Paul Ramsey. I knew it was a small program. They had room for three residents. They took six interns, but three of them were planning on going into specialties after the first year, so there was no competition for a residency spot. Also, the chairman of the surgery department, Dr. John Perry, had decided five years earlier that one of the three residents would be female, so that eliminated a lot of the prejudice against women going into surgery. I also think, in retrospect, that I was aware of the moral character of the program, but I didn't recognize it as such at the time. I really liked the program, and I liked the idea of going back to Minnesota.

After completing the interviews, each student lists his or her preference of residency programs as first choice, second choice, etc. Each residency program lists the students it has interviewed in order of preference. These lists are submitted to a computer in Evanston, Illinois, which matches students to residencies. The results of the "match" are made known at the same time on the same day throughout the United States. At the same time, a list of residencies that didn't fill is published so that any student who didn't match can call in the next few hours to find a place to go. St. Paul Ramsey was my first choice. Burlington, Vermont, was my second. I matched my first choice. My friend from college went into pediatrics and matched to Burlington, Vermont.

Ultimately, one of the interns from the year ahead of me at St. Paul Ramsey decided not to go into a specialty and wanted to stay on as a general surgery resident. That would eventually make four residents for three chief resident positions. The chairman of the department of surgery decided to accommodate him, but in order to give each resident a year as chief resident, he had to reduce the number of residents he took the following year. So, I was one of two general surgery interns accepted in 1976. It recently occurred to me to wonder how many medical students were considered for the position I got. I was able to ask one of the surgeons involved in the selection of residents, and he said they usually interviewed ten to twelve medical students.

So, I found myself scheduled to begin a surgery residency. It was at this point that I stopped to think about whether this was what I wanted to do for the rest of my life. Up until then, everything just seemed to happen. I don't remember consciously making any major life decisions. I had kept going to school because I liked school. I went to medical school because I did much better on the MCAT exam than on the GRE. I applied to research-oriented medical schools on the advice of my advisor and went to a school where my friend went. I chose surgery because it felt right, and my choice of residency was evident after my interviews. I had been making decisions but not stopping to think about them very much. I had just been following the course laid out before me. Now it seemed I had a very important decision to make before I went any further. I considered my abilities and history. I liked surgery. I thought surgery was something I could do and that I could do it well. I decided to become a surgeon.

I graduated from the Pritzker School of Medicine in May 1976. I paid for it through grants and scholarships, one of which was from the Robert Woods Johnson Foundation. Another I secured because I was a female interested in music. The rest of my financing came from loans. At the end of medical school, I was twenty-two thousand dollars in debt. (Today it is not uncommon for medical students to accumulate one hundred and fifty thousand to two hundred thousand dollars in debt for four years of college and four years of medical school.) Payment of school debt could be delayed during residency, so I didn't start paying on my school loans until I was in practice. I made my last payment in 1990.

3

Internship

Interns start at the end of June, one week before the other residents move up one position. As an intern, you are responsible for knowing all the patients on your service. It's your job to make sure all the work gets done. You don't make many decisions initially, but you do all the scut work. When I was an intern, there weren't any blood-drawing teams or IV teams. That was all done by the intern. It was very demanding, but I liked it.

At first I felt lost. I sometimes didn't understand what they were talking about on rounds; rounds are when all the residents on the service join the attending surgeon to see all the patients and discuss their diseases and treatments. There is a lot of lingo in surgery. In medical school, things were discussed in medical terms. Surgery was different. The surgical procedures are referred to by the developer's name, such as the McVay hernia repair, the Halsted mastectomy, etc. Also, many of the instruments and drains are named for someone. It's an Adson's, not a pick-up, or it's a Kelly clamp or Kocher clamp, or a Mayo scissors. It's a Foley catheter or a Penrose drain. I preferred names like "red rubber catheter." I knew right away what they were referring to when it was described this way. It certainly would be easier if they named an instrument by what it did or what it looked like. Also, the diseases were named after someone, such as Boerhaaves syndrome. I eventually began to pick up on the lingo. One day it all seemed to click, and I began to understand what they were talking about.

During my first year I did a rotating internship, which means I worked on a variety of services, including the emergency room (ER), internal medicine, obstetrics and gynecology, orthopedics, and surgery. I didn't like the ER. The major trauma patients were immediately transported to the operating room. They didn't even stop in the ER. I sewed up a lot of lacerations, sometimes almost without anesthesia because the patient was so drunk that he or she couldn't feel it. I saw one lady walk out of the ER on the end of her tibia (lower leg bone) with her foot off to the side, and it didn't seem to bother her at all. I was amazed she was still upright. Eventually, the smell of alcohol on someone's breath would make me sick to my stomach.

Once I was assigned to work up a man who had attempted suicide. After talking to him for a while, he had me convinced that he had no other choice but to do what he did. That situation was something I wasn't prepared for. We saw a lot of patients on drugs. One boy on PCP fought the police so hard that he broke his femur. It takes a lot of force to break that bone.

The worst case I attended was that of a two-year-old child presenting in complete arrest. The story was that she had been left in the care of her uncle. He had fallen asleep with his legs resting over her chest. When he woke up, she wasn't breathing, so he brought her to the ER by car. We worked on her for more than an hour and a half with no response to anything we did. When we finally quit, we examined her and found her privates all torn up. She had been sexually molested. I had a hard time dealing with that one. A month in the ER was enough for me.

I did a three-month rotation on internal medicine. What I remember most is caring for patients in the coronary care unit. One patient had such large varicose veins on his legs that you could take his pulse by standing at the foot of the bed and counting the pulse in his veins. Two patients that I cared for developed cardiac dysrhythmias following their heart attacks. Their hearts were going at very rapid rates and weren't pumping blood very well; their conditions would deteriorate if we didn't do something. We could attempt to correct their heart rate with a shock of low electrical current (as opposed to the high current we use for defibrillation). The patient would be sedated and given a shock via paddles placed on the chest. In both of my patients' cases, they converted to a normal rhythm as I held the paddles over their chests. I didn't even touch them. Perhaps it was the sedation, or perhaps I have a powerful aura. Word got around that I was "charged."

My month rotation on obstetrics and gynecology was a blur. I met my future husband that month, so my attention was directed elsewhere. I may have observed an abortion, but I had been told it was a D&C (Dilatation and Curretage). I do remember seeing a patient with toxic shock syndrome, a virulent staph infection of the pelvis associated with tampon use that develops rapidly and can lead to sepsis (infection of the blood stream), shock (low blood pressure and low cardiac output), and death.

Of course, the rotations I enjoyed the most were on the surgical services. I got to perform some surgeries. Appendectomies and hernia repairs were intern cases. At first, one is very slow in doing anything until learning how to do it. I remember one hernia case in which the attending surgeon left the room before I was finished because he said it was taking me too long. Years later, I watched a television program called *St. Elsewhere* where they showed the passage of time down in the corner of the screen. They portrayed a situation in which a hernia repair took four hours! My attending would never have tolerated that!

We got to scrub on the major cases, but usually only to hold a retractor up in a corner where you couldn't see what was going on. One such case I will always remember, not because of the patient, but because of what happened to me. The patient was a woman in her late twenties with recurrent ovarian cancer causing a bowel obstruction. She'd had at least one previous operation in the abdomen to remove tumors. When the abdomen was opened, it was obvious that everything was stuck together; it would all have to be carefully taken apart to see where the problem was to fix it. That was going to take several hours. I was assigned to hold the retractor in the right upper quadrant, above the operating resident. After four hours of operating, the nurses began to feel sorry for us interns and decided we needed some nourishment. The nurse slipped a piece of hard candy inside our masks and into our mouths. I tried to suck on it, but at one point I inadvertently bit down on it, and it stuck to one of the gold crowns I had on my molars. As I tried to move the candy, it pulled the crown off. I didn't know what to do. I was too embarrassed to ask to be excused from the case or to ask someone to take something out of my mouth. Before I could decide what to do, I accidentally swallowed the candy and the crown. The immediate problem was solved, and I was able to continue holding the retractor until they were done operating. Since it was a gold crown, though, I wanted to retrieve it. I watched for ten days for that crown to come through. I finally decided to get an X-ray to see if the crown was still inside so if it wasn't I could stop checking.

The OR scrubs we wore were zippered tunic tops with pants. The zipper went straight down the front. I didn't get undressed for a quick X-ray of my abdomen. On X-ray, we discovered that the crown was still inside, near the bottom, but to my surprise, I had scoliosis. My spine went from one side of the zipper to the other. I had never been diagnosed as having scoliosis before. I remember having backaches as a kid and that my folks took me to a chiropractor, but no one ever told me my spine was crooked.

I consulted an orthopedic surgeon who said that because of my age, nothing could be done to straighten my spine. It could have been addressed at an earlier age. He said it probably wouldn't bother me too much anyway. As I get older, I find it harder to reach one foot than the other, and I have a backache if I lean over the sink for any length of time, but otherwise I'm okay.

I finally retrieved the crown, and the dentist cleaned it up and put it back in place. I honestly don't remember how the patient did.

I spent a month on orthopedics as an intern. The case I remember most was a young woman who was involved in a motorcycle accident and had many injuries, including a fracture of her pelvis and fractures of her upper leg, her lower leg, and her ankle all on her left side. She was awake and alert. She had a positive peritoneal lavage, which meant that she was bleeding in her abdomen, so that took priority. She was taken to the OR for an abdominal exploration. Before she went to sleep, she kept asking if she was going to die, and we assured her that she wasn't. My concern was that I was going to be up all night fixing her fractures after they fixed whatever was wrong in her abdomen. When they got inside, there was a lot of blood. They found her liver completely torn away from all its vessels and attachments. They literally took her liver out of her abdomen and laid it on her chest. There was nothing they could do. She died.

Reducing hip dislocations is very hard because of the strength of the muscles surrounding the hip joint. I attempted reducing one under general anesthesia, which is what you have to do to get the muscles to relax. I stood on the operating table over the patient pulling up on the leg with all I was worth and still couldn't reduce it. I had to call the ortho resident. He was a big man and did it with ease.

I successfully completed my internship year and was ready to learn more about general surgery in my residency.

4

Residency

At St. Paul Ramsey, there were three surgical services—red was the trauma service, green was the general surgery service, and yellow was the burn service. There were six attending surgeons: Dr. John Perry, Dr. Frank Quattlebaum, Dr. Ronald Fischer, Dr. Albert Mowlem, Dr. Richard Strate, and Dr. Elmer Kasperson. They took turns being the attending on the surgical services. During our second and third years as residents, we did three-month rotations on the surgical services as well as a rotation each on pediatric surgery and neurosurgery.

St. Paul Ramsey Hospital (now known as Regions Medical Center) is located at the junction of I-94 and I-35E in St. Paul. When I was a resident, St. Paul Ramsey was known as a trauma hospital, and it got a lot of patients from accidents on the freeways. We also got a lot of gun and knife wounds, because we were the county hospital.

The way we handled trauma patients at St. Paul Ramsey was to take them immediately to the operating room. They were not evaluated in the ER. We had all the personnel and equipment to care for these patients in operating room 10. This operating room was kept open and available for just such patients. So when a trauma patient came into the ER either by ambulance or unexpectedly, the patient was taken to the OR. At the same time, an overhead page for "surgery stat to room 10" was heard. The surgery crew arrived in the OR about the same time as the patient. When you were on the "red surgery" service, you were thus paged to OR room 10 at least once a day. It got to be that at night, if I got a chance to sleep, the cadence of the page for "surgery stat to room 10" would wake me up even before the operator called the call room.

Anesthesia responded to the page and took care of the patient's airway. We had taped on the walls of the operating room protocols on how to manage various injuries. For instance, "How to manage a head injury." If it was serious, neurosurgery was available. We always assumed a neck fracture until it was ruled out by X-ray. Limb fractures were usually managed by the orthopedic surgery service. Pelvic fractures can be the cause of a large amount of blood loss, so they were evaluated and addressed by protocol to limit blood loss. Hematuria, blood in the urine, could be a sign of kidney damage, and we had a protocol to evaluate that. Severe bladder or kidney injuries were taken care of by urology. As general surgeons, we were in charge of coordinating all of the patient's care and, if necessary, operating on the chest and/or abdomen and repairing vascular injuries.

Dr. Perry, the chairman of the department of surgery, had authored several articles on how doing peritoneal lavages could help determine if there was intra-abdominal injury. It is very difficult in a trauma patient to determine if there is injury in the abdomen. Abdominal exams have been shown to be unreliable in patients who are awake, and most of the time our patients were unconscious. The best way to check for intra-abdominal injury (before ultrasound was readily available) was to do a peritoneal lavage.

Basically, you make a small incision in the midline of the abdomen just below the belly button. The incision goes through the fascia between the muscle layers of the abdominal wall, and a puncture is made through the peritoneum into the abdominal cavity.

A small catheter is placed into the abdomen so the tip is in the pelvis. An attempt is then made to aspirate any fluid. If a 10 cc syringe rapidly fills with red blood, the finding is positive, and the patient is prepped for abdominal exploration. If a little blood is aspirated, it may or may not be significant. To help determine if it is significant, one liter of saline solution is allowed to flow into the abdomen through the catheter and then allowed to flow out by gravity back into the bottle. A sample of the efflux is sent to the lab for evaluation. If the red cell or white cell counts are over a predetermined amount or if there is bile or amylase or food particles in the sample, it is considered positive, and the patient is prepped for surgery. If the counts are borderline, the catheter can be left in to take another sample later; in the meantime, the patient is observed. If the counts are very low, it is considered negative, and the catheter is removed. We did a lot of peritoneal lavages. It was the first procedure we got to do as interns, and as residents we coached all the subsequent interns through theirs.

During my fourth year of residency, one of the projects I did was to organize all the protocols for the care of the various injuries of trauma patients into a folder to give to the new residents. The now familiar ATLS (advanced trauma life support) material contains a lot of the same information.

I remember many patients from my residency rotations on the trauma service. One of the first was a patient I met in the clinic. He was a young man who had been shot in the heart. He had been successfully operated on emergently, and his life had been saved. He complained about his scar! He had a scar from the pubic bone (the base of his penis) up the midline to his sternal notch. I, for the first time, understood what "from stem to stern" meant.

I was involved with another patient who presented to room 10 with a gunshot wound to the heart. My senior resident was a small woman. She took the knife and made an incision in the fifth intercostal space (between the ribs) on the left to get at the heart, but she couldn't move the ribs to get the retractor in. I stepped in and pulled the ribs apart, breaking several of them as I did it. I didn't realize I was so strong, but my adrenaline was pumping.

One patient was a large black man who had been shot in the chest with a .22 caliber rifle. We took an X-ray and saw the bullet in the left chest, but the patient was awake and alert, his vital signs were normal, and he didn't have a pneumothorax—air around the lung. No treatment was necessary except observation to see if anything developed. The man's wife was not satisfied with us just watching her husband. She wanted the bullet out. We explained to her that we would be doing more damage trying to get the bullet out than what he had suffered in getting shot. She finally was okay with our approach. He did well. So much for taking the bullet out as they always did in the movie Westerns.

We dealt with innumerable victims of motorcycle accidents. The first thing we always did to evaluate a trauma patient was to get rid of all the clothes so we could see where the injuries were. Out of all the patients we cared for, I can recall only one occasion where we had to cut through a leather coat or leggings. Not many of the motorcycle accident victims wore leather protection. We did have to cut through chains and remove a lot of jewelry from piercings.

One of the motorcycle accident victims that I was responsible for in room 10 had a severe head injury. He was eventually pronounced brain dead and was the donor for the first heart transplant performed at the University of Minnesota Hospital.

I remember a young female who was on a motorcycle with her husband when they were in an accident. She had multiple fractures and a severe chest injury but no head injury. Her lungs were so badly damaged that they progressed to developing what is called ARDS—acute respiratory distress syndrome. We had her on a ventilator at the maximum settings with maximum PAP (positive airway pressure). We had two chest tubes in each side of her chest, and she was still deteriorating. We were considering putting her on oxygen membrane support (a machine to put oxygen into the blood), which was very new at that time and used mostly in infants. The next day there were small signs of improvement. She rallied, and her lungs healed. We all had champagne the day she came off the ventilator. She was in the intensive care unit a long time, and I am sure it took her a long time to recover from her injuries. It is said that for every day you are in bed, it takes you a week to gain your strength back. She was in bed for at least a month. That would mean it would have taken her thirty weeks, or more than half a year, to get her strength back. Wow!

We also cared for many victims of car accidents. Most of their injuries were considered blunt trauma injuries as opposed to penetrating trauma, which would be from a gun shot or stabbing. One of the most severe, life-threatening injuries you can get from a rapid deceleration car accident is a ruptured thoracic aorta. The arch of the aorta, the main artery coming off of the heart, sits freely in the chest until it comes to an area in the left chest where it becomes attached to the surrounding tissues in the back, near the back bone. In a rapid deceleration accident—a sudden stop—the arch of the aorta continues to move forward, but the part attached to the other tissues can't move and can tear at that point. Most patients with this type of injury don't make it to the hospital because they bleed out so fast. A few patients may present with this injury, but it has to be diagnosed early and treated in order for them to survive. It is a difficult diagnosis to make. Dr. Perry had authored several articles on X-ray findings that would make you suspect your patient had a ruptured thoracic aorta, and we were drilled on these frequently.

I remember a young man who was brought to the hospital following a bad motorcycle accident on a Friday night. He had multiple fractures, including a pelvic fracture. Orthopedics operated on him for many hours that night to put his bones back together. He appeared to be doing okay post-op. We reviewed his X-rays with the radiologist on Monday afternoon. (We didn't have radiology coverage on the weekend and were expected to read our own X-rays in real time. We reviewed all the X-rays on patients that had come in over the weekend with the radiologist on Monday afternoons.) On reviewing the chest X-ray, the radiologist pointed out findings that raised the suspicion of a ruptured aorta. We had missed them. But how could this be? The patient had survived for three days and prolonged surgery with good vital signs.

We did an angiogram, and sure enough, he had a ruptured thoracic aorta. He was a young man, eighteen years old, and apparently the surrounding tissues had held the ends of the torn aorta close enough together to allow sufficient blood to flow past the hole to support his circulation. We took him to the operating room and repaired the tear with a graft. During the procedure, we had to bypass the blood around the area where we were working by using a shunt, which was removed once the graft was in place. The patient did well post-op and was sent to the orthopedic floor for care of his fractures. Several days later, the area on the artery in the neck where we had temporarily placed the shunt blew out, and we had to go back to the OR emergently. That one bled very fast. We were able to repair that hole, and he subsequently went on to recover without further problem. That patient defied all the odds and survived despite us. I think he was meant to live.

Many of the car accident victims had head injuries. If a patient had a severe head injury, he or she needed a CT scan to determine the extent of the injury. Early in my residency, our hospital didn't have a CT scanner, but a nearby hospital did. We would intubate the patient and transport him or her by ambulance to the other hospital for the scan and then come back to St. Paul Ramsey for care. During all of this moving, it was the resident's responsibility to bag or breathe for the patient, keep the breathing tube in place, and keep all the IVs intact. I was sure glad when we got our own CT scanner.

Hospitals began using criteria to pronounce someone brain dead during the 1970s. I remember a twelve-year-old boy who had been in a car accident and had suffered a severe brain injury. There was no evidence of any brain activity at all, and he was pronounced brain dead after meeting all the required criteria. Everyone agreed we should turn off the ventilator. Once the family was gathered, I turned the breathing machine off. The patient was still on the cardiac monitor, and even though he wasn't breathing, his heart kept right on beating. It slowed down, but it didn't stop. After ten minutes, I turned the heart monitor off because I couldn't watch it anymore. I remember thinking how hard this had to be for the family.

Other trauma patients we cared for included a young man who had attempted suicide by jumping off a cliff onto the railroad tracks and then was hit by the train. He survived. We called him Superman.

Another young lady jumped off of a bridge. She landed on her back on the water and wasn't injured except for bruising down her entire back side. When she walked down the hall with her gown open in the back, her butt cheeks would slosh back and forth from the liquefied blood in them.

Once I put a chest tube in a large man with a hemopneumothorax (blood and air around the lung). As I slipped the large tube in, he coughed with such force that the blood spurted across the room and onto the wall before I could connect the tube to the suction unit. That surprised everyone!

When I was a junior resident, I was called back to the hospital to help one night because they had three room 10s already going, and another one was on the way in. I was put in charge of the fourth patient. I did the initial evaluation and had a positive peritoneal lavage. I was instructed to open the abdomen and find out what was bleeding. I did an exploration and discovered a ruptured spleen. I had to put pressure on the spleen to slow the bleeding the best I could until the chief resident could come and help me remove it. The patient did well.

One of the most tenuous cases involved a man who had been involved in a boating accident. He apparently had run his boat up onto land in the middle of the night. Why he was traveling so fast in a boat at night I don't know. We found a bad liver injury. To repair the liver, we would take pieces of the omentum, an apron of fat inside the abdomen, and use them to buttress the stitches so they wouldn't pull through the liver as they were tied. The liver tears easily and bleeds a lot. We would work for a while until the blood pressure would start to fall and then would pack the liver and hold pressure on it until anesthesia caught up with the fluid and blood loss. One person would stay scrubbed and hold the liver while the others would go get some refreshments. When the blood pressure was stable again, they would scrub back in and work some more. We worked for twelve hours on that patient and finally got the bleeding to stop. Post-operatively, we drew blood to do some tests to see where we were. The blood samples were so diluted they looked like red Kool-Aid. We didn't expect him to survive. The next morning on our rounds, we found him awake, sitting up in bed, and wondering what had happened.

Once I was assisting another resident with repairing a large scalp laceration on a very intoxicated woman. We were standing above her head out of her eye sight. She kept moaning "Oh God, oh God," over and over again. It got to be annoying. Finally the male resident responded to her by saying, "Yeeess" in a low, drawnout voice. She quit moaning and didn't say anything for the rest of the time we were sewing her up.

St. Paul Ramsey Medical Center was the burn center for a large area of the Midwest. Patients with major burns or burns of the face, hands, or perineum from Minnesota, Wisconsin, South Dakota, and North Dakota were transferred to us for care. We would get a call from a local doctor and advise him or her on the initial care and how to transport the patient. If a patient was coming from a long way away, we would fly out in a small Cessna plane. Sometimes we would have to fly around the water towers to identify the town we were looking for.

In burn patients, the initial fluid resuscitation is critical. They sequester a tremendous amount of fluid in the burned skin, and if you don't keep up with the fluid loss, the patient will go into kidney failure. We lost one little girl because the local MD didn't believe she needed the amount of fluid we recommended. There is a basic universal formula that is used to calculate how much fluid a patient needs, and it is critical that the patient gets it.

Back in the late 1970s, we cared for burns by dressing them with silvadene cream with daily dressing changes. If the patient was ambulatory, the dressing would be changed in a big tub. I remember one young boy who each morning would walk to the tub room crying. He would scream during the dressing change and debridement. Only general anesthesia would relieve the pain, and we didn't want to do that every day. The nurses encouraged the patients to voice their pain.

Once he was redressed, he was okay, and the rest of the day he would walk around the unit and bother the nurses. The next day he would walk to the tub room again crying, but he'd be going on his own. He did not have to be cajoled. I don't know if I could do that.

We cared for an eighteen-year-old boy who was involved in a car accident after partying the night of high school graduation. He was burned very badly. Part of his skull was exposed and charred. After resuscitation and debridement, we began trying to cover the burn areas with some of his remaining skin. We would harvest skin and then mesh it nine-to-one to stretch it to cover as much as possible. We worked on him for months.

Burn patients are very susceptible to infections, so we started them on antibiotics at the first sign of infection. We would treat them with one antibiotic for a while, and then a different infection, caused by a bacteria resistant to that antibiotic, would show up, so we would then treat that one with another antibiotic. It was a race to see if we could get a patient covered with skin before he or she developed an infection that was resistant to all our antibiotics.

We appeared to be doing okay with this young man until one day I noticed that the front shin areas on his lower legs were fluctuant, as if they were fluid and not solid as muscle should be. We discovered he had abscesses in both anterior compartments of his lower legs. The bacteria involved was methicillin-resistant staphylococcus (MRS), a hard one to treat. We debrided his legs, but we couldn't clear the infection, and he died.

We feared MRS. We, as residents, were cultured to make sure we weren't carriers of the bacteria. My nose cultured positive once, so I had to put anti-bacterial cream in my nose twice a day for several weeks to clear it up.

Doing rounds on the burn unit required changing gowns, masks, and gloves before going into each patient's room so that we wouldn't contaminate one patient with the bacteria another patient had.

A simple formula we used to determine the survival of a burn patient was to add the body surface area of the burn and the age of the patient. That sum was their mortality rate in most cases.

A forty-year-old male patient presented with a 100 percent body-surface-area burn. He was awake and alert and breathing on his own. Before we intubated him (the tissues in his airway had also been burnt and were swelling and would soon close), we explained to him the situation and gave him the option of no treatment. He chose no treatment and died shortly thereafter.

One patient was a poster child for good burn care who defied his mortality odds. He was a nineteen-year-old man who had suffered a 90 percent body-surface-area burn—everything was burned except his head (90 + 19 = 109 percent mortality). They had been able to resurface his entire body by harvesting skin from his head in stages. He came back while I was on the burn unit for release of some contractures he had developed as the skin healed and contracted under his arms and in the groin.

We cared for electrical burns as well. An injured lineman was brought in one day with a severe electrical burn. I peeked into the OR where they were treating him. I could only see his legs, but all I saw was charred bone. I wasn't involved in his initial care, but later in the week, it was my responsibility to draw blood samples on the patients in the burn unit. He apparently was one of the patients on my list. I didn't know his name, so I didn't recognize it. As I approached the next patient on my list, I noticed he was lying in a water bed. I hadn't seen a water bed before, so I was curious as to how it worked. He appeared to be sunk into the bed, and I just about said,

"In that bed it almost looks like you don't have any legs." I suddenly realized who he was and bit my tongue before I spoke. It was the lineman, and he didn't have any legs. They had been amputated.

Near the end of my residency, a patient came in who had been riding a motorcycle and was hit by a pickup. The pickup driver wasn't aware of the accident and had dragged the motorcyclist a quarter of a mile down the blacktop before he stopped. The motorcyclist had on a leather jacket and chaps, but dragging him down the blacktop like that had sanded off the left side of his body. Half his arm was gone, and you could see right into the elbow joint. The outer half of his leg was gone, and there was gravel ground into the remaining tissue and bone. He had lost so much of his body surface area that we treated him like a burn patient. We debrided his wounds in the OR for a long time. I don't know what his outcome was.

Burns are treated differently now than they were in the 1970s. Early active debridement with immediate grafting is done on most burns now. We did that only on critical areas like the face, hands, and perineum. There is a whole assortment of artificial skin products available now for initial coverage. As I said earlier, the faster you get coverage, the fewer infections. The best thing you can do for burns is to prevent them in the first place!

The specialty of neurosurgery deals with patients with strokes, head injuries, spinal cord and nerve injuries, tumors, and nerve-entrapment syndromes. We didn't do much with stroke patients, but we saw a lot of head injuries. When I was a resident, neurosurgeons started using intracranial pressure monitoring, a means to measure pressure inside the head in head injury patients. The brain has a limited way to respond to injury—it swells. And since it is in a confined place, the swelling causes a pressure increase. If the pressure in the head exceeds the venous blood pressure, it stops blood flow out of the brain. If the pressure is high enough, it will cause the brain to herniate out the bottom of the skull and put pressure on critical nerves and on the brain stem, which controls breathing. We could do several things to lower pressure in the head if it was getting too high. We could raise the head of the bed and reduce IV fluids, we could decrease the carbon dioxide in the blood by hyperventilating the patient, and we could give the patient steroids. If these measures didn't do enough, a piece of the skull could be removed temporarily and the skin closed over the brain to give it more room.

To measure the pressure inside the head, we used a small device that looked like a spark plug, an intracranial pressure monitor. We would place this device by making a small skin incision under local anesthesia in one of the skin lines of the forehead. (I don't know why we did it on the forehead. Later they were placed behind the hair line so the scar wasn't visible.) Then a small hole was drilled through the skull with a two-handed hand drill. The pressure device was then screwed into the skull, and a large needle was used to poke a hole in the dura—the lining inside the skull. Tubing from the device was connected to a manometer, and the pressure was measured. It had to be done with the head at the same elevation for every reading. This was very high tech—a spark plug, a hand drill, poke a hole, etc. I don't know how well they worked, but I liked the procedure.

One serious head-injury patient woke up after being comatose for several months. Brain injury takes a long time to heal, and function doesn't return until the healing process reaches a critical point. The healing can take a year or longer. You can't predict how any particular patient will do.

One day the neurosurgeon was over at the University of Minnesota when a patient arrived with a subdural hematoma. The treatment for this is to do a craniotomy to take out the blood clot. I consulted with the neurosurgeon, and he told me to get started with the case and he would be there soon. Up until that time, the only thing I had done was shave patients' heads with the straight razor. I had assisted on several craniotomies, and the neurosurgeon obviously thought I knew what to do, so I proceeded. I prepped and draped the patient after he was put to sleep. I drilled the holes in the skull and cut out a piece of the skull by connecting the holes with a saw. I took off the skull and cut open the dura. I took out the blood clot and the brain started to swell very rapidly. The neurosurgeon wasn't there yet. I didn't know what to do. The brain was swelling out of the hole so far I was afraid the tissue would tear on the cut edges of the skull. The only thing I could think of to do was to put my hand on the brain and try to hold it in. That wasn't very successful. I knew what was happening wasn't good for the patient, but I didn't know of anything else to do. The neurosurgeon finally arrived, and all we did was sew the skin back together to cover the brain. The patient didn't wake up, and I learned that that was typical for subdural hematoma patients.

I recently read a science fiction novel in which characters were keeping a severed head alive. They had removed the top of the skull and thought it was increasing in knowledge because the brain was swelling over the edges of the skull. Sorry, but that's not what was happening. The brain is just doing what it does when it is injured.

We also took care of patients with spinal cord injuries. I helped care for two patients with cervical neck fractures injuring the spinal cord. These patients can be paralyzed from the neck down. Some can breathe on their own; others cannot. We treated them by stabilizing the spinal bones with either a metal halo around the head externally (screwed into the skull) and applying traction, or surgically by screwing metal plates to the bones to keep them in place. Patients were placed on a circular bed that allowed us to turn them from lying on their backs to lying on their fronts without lifting them and disturbing the bones. If the bones moved, they could cause more damage to the spinal cord. Initially the spinal cord, like the brain, would swell from the injury. Once the swelling went down, we could begin to determine the level of loss of function. One patient was doing well until suddenly one day his blood pressure dropped. It didn't look like he had an infection. Perhaps his adrenal function had suddenly deteriorated for some reason. Perhaps he needed more fluids. Perhaps he had developed some cardiac problem and his heart wasn't working right. We rapidly gave him steroids to compensate for adrenal insufficiency and fluids for a possible fluid loss and did an EKG to check his heart. It turned out that what he needed was the fluids. He had reached a point in his recovery where the swelling in the spinal cord had gone down enough to allow the peripheral vessels to finally relax, so more fluid began to go to his legs. That opened up a large pool for blood to go to, and he needed more to fill it up. I was surprised it happened so suddenly.

Another patient with a potential spinal cord injury presented as a young boy with a large serrated knife stuck in his back. His mother had apparently stabbed him. He wasn't bleeding much. We were in room 10, so we were in the best place to handle whatever we needed to do when we pulled the knife out. The anesthetist put the patient to sleep and had to intubate the patient with him lying on his side. We then laid the patient on his stomach and started to work on the knife. Initially it wouldn't budge. We didn't want to move the knife around much, fearing we would be cutting nerves or the spinal cord if we did. We pushed it up a little bit and then pulled it down just a little bit, and by gentle, small movements we were eventually able to get the knife out. Everything remained stable. No gush of blood, no drop in blood pressure. On final evaluation, he was very lucky. All that was cut were some lateral spinal nerves that provided sensation to his side. We expected over time the surrounding nerves would cover most of the area that had lost sensation. Dealing with the fact that his mother had stabbed him would be the injury that would require the most treatment.

On the general surgery service, a resident did a wide variety of procedures. Common cases included appendectomies, hernia repairs, breast biopsies and surgeries, gall bladder removals, the removal of other lumps and bumps, amputations, and gastrostomies. We frequently put in chest tubes.

I remember one night we did three appendectomies. The second one was on one of our own residents. On the third case, we found a normal appendix and couldn't find anything else wrong in the abdomen. It turned out that that patient had renal failure and his pain was from that. We had neglected to do a urinalysis on him pre-op. Back then we did not perform CT scans to make the diagnosis of appendicitis; the diagnosis was based on the clinical findings. That case impressed upon me the importance of doing a urinalysis on every patient with abdominal pain.

Hernia repairs were primary repairs. There were no mesh plugs. All gall bladder surgeries were open procedures. Dr. Perry had a resting tremor, so when he assisted on a case and held retractors for exposure, the whole field would shake. When he put in a stitch, the tremor would go away. He always told us to say during board exams that we put in a drain in every gallbladder case, but we never did.

We did a lot of breast biopsies. Most breast surgery for cancer was a modified radical mastectomy. They were just beginning to do partial mastectomies/lumpectomies with follow-up irradiation near the end of my residency. We did a few radical mastectomies if the tumor had invaded the underlying muscle and/or bone. I remember one patient who had a mastectomy for breast cancer. She and her husband had been missionaries to China and were now retired. On rounds one day, post-op, she said her husband had given her a new name. She was now "One Hung Low."

One patient I remember very well, even though we didn't operate on her. She was a transfer from a small hospital in Wisconsin with the diagnosis of a ruptured abdominal aorta. Patients arriving with that diagnosis were taken immediately to room 10 just like trauma patients because they are so critical. She arrived awake and alert and conscious of what was going on. We started our usual evaluation and preparation for surgery. Since she was awake, and these patients usually weren't, I thought it would be appropriate to share with her what we were doing. When she heard that we were preparing for surgery, she said she didn't want that. She said "No!" Up until this point, she had lived alone and was very functional. She didn't want to possibly be paralyzed or have renal failure or be dependent in a nursing home. We honored her decision and took her to a regular hospital room on the surgical floor. Her family arrived shortly thereafter, and she passed away several hours later. The situation made quite an impression on me. Just because we could do the surgery, should we? I had never thought that we had a choice before.

Another patient we took care of for a long time was an older lady with Boerhaaves syndrome. She suffered a tear at the lower end of her esophagus caused by vomiting. Saliva and gastric juices leaked into her chest cavity around the lung. The condition is very rare, and it was several days before the diagnosis was made. During that time, the juices caused a considerable amount of damage. We drained the chest cavity with a chest tube. In order to allow the esophageal tissues to heal so we could do a repair, we had to bypass the area of the damage. That meant that we had to bring the upper esophagus out the side of the neck so no saliva could go down. We put a collection bag on that. We had to drain the stomach so no gastric juice could go up and get to the injured area, so we created a gastrostomy—a drain out of the stomach. We put a collection bag on that, also. Then, since we weren't able to feed her through the esophagus or the stomach, we had to feed her through a large IV and eventually through a feeding tube placed into the small bowel beyond the stomach. She was in this condition for at least two months in the hospital before any attempt at repair. Her attitude was amazing. She tolerated whatever we had to do. Eventually we were able to put things together, and everything worked.

My three-month rotation on pediatric surgery was at Children's Hospital in St. Paul. We did a lot of inguinal hernia repairs. We didn't put in an IV. The patients were put to sleep with a mask, and we worked rapidly. In children, you only have to find the hernia sac and tie it off. There is no defect in the floor of the inguinal canal that needs to be repaired as in an adult. Other pediatric cases included treatment for pyloric stenosis, undescended testicles, and abdominal tumors. I remember one premature infant who had a patent ductus arteriosus. That is the shunt used in utero to bypass the lungs since the oxygen is coming from the placenta. After birth, it is supposed to close so the blood goes through the lungs for oxygenation. In this little guy it didn't close, so we needed to tie it off. The patient was the size of my hand. The operation was done under heating lamps to keep the baby warm. We had to make an incision between the ribs on the left to get to the ductus. It didn't take long, and the patient did very well. Today they use medications to close the ductus.

Call was every third night initially, but for most of my residency, it was every fourth night. The night after you were on call, you were on back-up call in case those on call got overwhelmed with patients. I was called back only once. Since Dr. Perry selected a female resident every year, it wasn't unusual for the entire on-call surgical crew on any given night at St. Paul Ramsey to be entirely female, from chief resident to junior resident, to intern, to medical student. That was very rare in the 1970s. There was no prejudice at St. Paul Ramsey against female surgeons.

One year of residency is spent doing research. I did a research project under the direction of a cardiac surgeon. The experiment was to test the strength of different types of repairs for dissection of the thoracic aorta. The experiment was performed on dogs. The dog was anesthetized, and the chest was opened. A dissection of the aortic wall was created, similar to what happens in a diseased aorta. The aorta was repaired with a graft. When the repair was finished, medications were administered intravenously to raise the blood pressure to see if the repair would hold. The dog was then sacrificed, and the aorta was collected for microscopic examination. The goal of the experiment was to find out which repair was the best. It also gave me an opportunity to practice my surgical skills.

I also did a chart review study and published the results. We studied stomach injury from blunt abdominal trauma. I reviewed charts of trauma patients who had been treated at St. Paul Ramsey Hospital between January 1, 1966, and December 31, 1980. Only sixteen patients were identified that had sustained stomach injury from blunt trauma. We found that the stomach was injured due to blunt trauma only when it was very full at the time of the accident. When the stomach is distended, it becomes exposed below the rib cage on the left and becomes a larger target for injury than when it is empty. If the injury was identified early and repaired quickly, the patients did well.

Norwich Eaton Pharmaceutical Company funded a study I did assessing the nutritional needs of patients with severe head injury. In 1979, we were just beginning to recognize the influence of nutrition on recovery from injury. The study involved enrolling patients with severe head injury and no other injuries. We documented the patient's nutritional status when initially admitted and again after a period of time. Blood and urine samples were obtained and anthropometric measurements taken (measurements of how much muscle the patient had). Urine nitrogen measurements were used to determine protein breakdown. Then a formula was used to calculate caloric needs. A high-calorie feeding was begun as soon as there was evidence of gut function. Head injury patients proved to need approximately twice the caloric intake of a noninjured person. We concluded that the nutritional status of these patients should be monitored closely and that adequate nutritional support should be instituted as early as possible to decrease morbidity and shorten rehabilitation.

Another resident did a research study on splenic auto-transplantation. We frequently had to remove the spleen because of injury. It had been discovered that besides filtering the blood, which the liver did also, the spleen played a significant role in immunity, especially in young patients against pneumococcal pneumonia. The resident wondered if implanted splenic tissue from the removed spleen would grow and produce the elements of immunity. In patients who had to have their spleens removed, to control bleeding, we placed slices of spleen tissue in a pocket we created between the underside of the rectus muscle and the abdominal lining. It worked. Now much effort is used to not remove the spleen at all. Patients with splenic injuries are watched, and the spleen is allowed to heal itself. Few patients bleed enough to require removal of the spleen. The condition of the spleen is monitored by CT scans.

One other study was comparing sutures to staples in the closure of wounds. Staples were the new thing. My husband was part of this study. He had his gallbladder removed, and half of the incision was closed with sutures and half with staples. I think the half with the staples healed better. Several years later, I was paging through a surgical journal and was surprised when I recognized a picture of my husband's abdominal scar. Then I realized it was the article publishing the results of the study.

5

Chief Resident

I was the last resident of the St. Paul Ramsey Residency Training Program. In the 1970s everyone thought there was going to be a surplus of surgeons, so some surgery residency programs were closing. Dr. Perry anticipated that the program at St. Paul Ramsey would not survive, so he chose to affiliate with the University of Minnesota before he was forced to close. That occurred the year after I started my surgery training. The other resident who I started with quit the training program during our internship year, so that left me as the last resident.

For the four years of my residency training, all the residents ahead of me were St. Paul Ramsey residents, and all the residents behind me were University of Minnesota residents. The residents from the university were of a different kind. The university program was a pyramid program, which meant there were more residents than there were positions the next year, so there was fierce competition between the residents for those positions. At St. Paul Ramsey, the residents were like one big family. One of the junior residents I worked with as a chief resident eventually became the chairman of the department of surgery at the University of Minnesota.

As chief resident, I was responsible for everything that occurred on my surgical service. I was responsible for the care of every patient. I supervised the interns and junior residents in their care of patients pre-op and post-op and assisted them with their surgical procedures. The attending surgeon was available if I needed help.

I did the major cases with the assistance of the attending surgeon. There were few surgical specialties, no vascular surgeons or colorectal surgeons or thoracic surgeons. We did it all except for cardiac and transplant. I did mastectomies; colon resections; gallbladder removals with common bile duct explorations; exploratory laparotomies (non-trauma) for bowel obstructions, tumors, and cancers; gastrectomies and/or vagotomies for patients with peptic ulcers; other stomach surgeries for tumors/cancers; thoracotomies; vascular surgeries; and gastric bypasses.

When on call, I did the emergency surgery cases, mostly trauma. We'd evaluate the patient in room 10 and, if necessary, open the chest or abdomen to find out what the problem was. The attending physician was made aware that we were opening the abdomen or chest but didn't come in unless I wanted him to. We did a lot of trauma surgery and usually were up all night during our nights on call. We cared for victims of motor vehicle accidents, motorcycle accidents, stabbings, gunshot wounds, falls, and fights.

I liked trauma. Opening the abdomen was like opening a Christmas present. You never knew what you were going to find. We had a systematic way of exploring the abdomen to identify the injuries without missing anything. It was fun.

While we were in the OR, we were also responsible for the patients in the surgical intensive care unit and all the surgical patients on the surgical ward. The year I was chief resident, a cardiac surgeon from the University of Minnesota decided to do open-heart operations at St. Paul Ramsey Medical Center. He would come with his residents to do the cases, and then they would leave and it would become our responsibility to care for their patients post-op. Post-op cardiac surgery patients are very sick people. They are intubated and have chest tubes, and some of them are on intra-aortic balloon pumps to support their blood pressure. They require very close monitoring. That was difficult because we were in the operating room caring for trauma patients. The stress was apparently too much for me, as I developed an ulcer. I didn't have any pain, but I had some bleeding. Over one weekend I vomited a large amount of dark red material, and my stools were black. The only time I recall feeling ill was just before I vomited. On Monday I saw a physician, and I was admitted to the hospital urgently. I was put in the medical intensive care unit. I remember the intern whose job it was to put in my IV. She was very nervous. My situation required a large bore IV because there was the possibility of needing a blood transfusion. As the surgical chief resident, I was the one they usually called upon if they couldn't get an IV into a patient. And now this poor intern had to put an IV into me. She did a good job.

My workup included an upper GI X-ray and upper endoscopy. They did them both the same morning. They didn't see anything of significance, but the meds they gave me for the endoscopy slowed everything down so that the barium from the upper GI X-ray didn't move. I got to vomit the thick white stuff over and over again. I never bled again, I didn't need a transfusion, and I was discharged after about forty-eight hours.

Thereafter, they paid a University of Minnesota resident to "babysit" the cardiac surgery patients their first two nights post-op. The resident sat in the room with the patient and took care of all the patient's needs.

I did a number of vascular cases, though none stick out as anything special. I do remember that Dr. Perry commented on my small, even stitches when sewing vessels back together. I believe that was because of all the practice I'd had sewing my own clothes and hemming dish towels in 4-H.

I did a few gastric bypasses for obesity, but we did more re-do operations on bypass patients for complications.

One of the benefits of being the chief resident was that I occasionally got to go with Dr. Perry and Dr. Strate to do surgery in Amery, Wisconsin. That gave me an opportunity to see what it was going to be like to practice in a small rural community. During one of those trips, I learned that Dr. Perry had said that I was a good surgeon and would be successful at whatever I did. That was very encouraging.

Throughout your residency, the surgery department keeps a record of all the cases you do—those where you are the primary surgeon, those you assist on, and all the cases that you help others with. It is very interesting at this point in my life to review the list and see what kinds of surgery I did then.

Since I was the last resident of the St. Paul Ramsey Surgery Residency Training Program, the surgery department had a big party for me when I finished. I still have the briefcase they gave me as a gift.

After completing my five years of surgical residency training, I wanted to rest for a while, so I took three months off. I worked a few hours a week in an emergency room in a hospital in a northern suburb of Minneapolis where I had done some moonlighting. I had worked there when I was off duty at St. Paul Ramsey, mostly during the year I was in the research lab. I took the ACLS (advanced cardiac life support) course, so I knew what to do for heart attack patients. I did all right with taking care of pediatric patients by depending on the nurses and the parents. One pediatric patient with hyperparathyroidism presented in crisis. I did what the parents told me to do because they knew much more about the disease than I did.

I knew how to take care of trauma patients, but I was limited as to what I could do in the ER. I would do the initial assessment and stabilization and then would call in the specialists to do the definitive care. These were specialists in private practice, and I was surprised when they would tell me to call someone else to care for the patient. For example, I had a patient with a bad laceration of the brachial artery in the armpit, the main artery to the arm. He was bleeding rather rapidly. I called the vascular surgeon, and he told me to call the general surgeon. I called the general surgeon, and he told me to call the vascular surgeon. I couldn't get anyone to come in to see the patient!

I had always planned on becoming board certified, so when I finished residency I asked what I had to do to make that happen. I found out that it wasn't up to me. The chairman of the department of surgery had to notify the American Board of Surgery that I had successfully completed a year of chief residency. He also had to provide a copy of the list of procedures I had done. If the paperwork was in order and approved, the American Board of Surgery would then invite me to take the written exam. I had to pass the written exam to qualify to take the oral exam, and if I passed that, I became board certified. Each candidate has three tries to pass these exams. If you are unsuccessful after three tries, you have to repeat a year of residency to be eligible to try again. Just a little pressure! There was a substantial fee for each exam. I spent some of my time during my three months off studying for the written exam.

6

My First Job

Since I was from Minnesota, my first choice for a job was a small community in Minnesota. I preferred northern Minnesota, but there weren't any job openings for a general surgeon there at the time. I learned of one surgeon who provided surgical services to several small towns in northwest Minnesota. His wife would drive him from hospital to hospital in their station wagon while he slept in the back. I didn't want to work like that. All the other small towns had their own surgeon, and none of them would be retiring soon.

I was offered a position in Amery, Wisconsin, the small town where I went as a resident, but I would still be affiliated with St. Paul Ramsey, and I didn't want to do that. I checked out a position in Flagstaff, Arizona. I wasn't offered the job. I interviewed for a position in Spooner, Wisconsin, and in Devil's Lake, North Dakota. I took the position in Devil's Lake, basically because they offered more money. That seemed to be the most important criteria for my husband, who was acting as my agent. I joined the clinic there in October 1981.

Devil's Lake, North Dakota, is about ninety miles west of Grand Forks. The population at the time was about seven thousand. The land is flat with few trees, and it seems to always be windy. It was my impression that people didn't live there because they wanted to live there. They lived there because they couldn't get out.

The hospital was run by a group of nuns. There were fourteen physicians in the clinic, including one surgeon, one urologist/surgeon, one cardiologist, and eleven family practitioners. I was the only female physician. I assisted the other surgeon a lot, but that was good. Soon after I finished residency, I ran across an article published in 1979 that listed the top ten operations performed in the United States. I had just finished five years of surgical training and planned to practice in a rural setting, and I was trained to do only four of them. I wasn't prepared. However, I learned how to do C-sections, tubal ligations, D&Cs, laparoscopies, and hysterectomies from the other surgeon in Devil's Lake.

It seemed the only surgical cases that were mine were those that presented when I was on call. All the family practice physicians continued to refer their cases to the surgeon they were familiar with. When I was on call, I was required to see all trauma patients who came to the ER. I was called in for every laceration or injury. I wasn't very busy except on the nights I was on call for the ER.

The clinic rules were that I had to be at the clinic a certain number of hours each day, even if I didn't have anything to do. I clocked in and out on a time card. I started doing women's health just to keep busy. I did a lot of female exams, including those on the nuns who ran the hospital.

I did have a couple of interesting cases. I had put in pacemakers during residency, which was a service they hadn't been able to provide in Devil's Lake before my arrival. A patient presented with a very slow heart beat and needed a pacemaker. We successfully placed the pacemaker, and the patient went on to become the bridge champion at the nursing home. The story made the front page of the local paper.

Another patient came to see me because she had had an abdominal surgery by the urologist/surgeon about a year earlier, and she was concerned that one side of her abdomen now stuck out more than the other side. We did X-rays and a CT scan, and there was a mass, possibly a sponge, on the right side of the scar, just inside her abdominal wall. I took her to the OR and found a large sponge walled off in its own cavity. We removed it, and she recovered without further problem. She did sue the other surgeon, but I believe he died of cancer before it was settled.

We were in Devil's Lake only five months before we started looking for another job. I wasn't getting to do much surgery. I had done five years of surgery training to do surgery, not to repair lacerations and perform female exams. My husband didn't like it there, as it was cold. It was so cold that there was a plugin for your car in the clinic parking lot so you could warm up the engine block of your car so it would start at the end of the day. And to top it off, the financial arrangement wasn't what we had understood it to be.

I looked at an opportunity in Appleton, Wisconsin, and I looked at Amery again. Eventually I saw an ad in the *Journal of the American Medical Association* about the need for a surgeon in Sparta, Wisconsin. We answered the ad. We visited Sparta during Thanksgiving week. The locals were deer hunting in T-shirts; it was that warm. Though geographically it wasn't much further south than Devil's Lake, it appeared to be much nicer weather.

The then-president of the Sparta Clinic was in a Milwaukee hospital recovering from open-heart surgery, so after I returned to North Dakota, the clinic administrator arranged a three-way conference call so he could talk to me. He apparently said after our conversation, "Any woman who could finish a surgery residency must be good." I got the job. We left Devil's Lake, North Dakota, in a snowstorm at the end of December 1982.

7

Sparta, Wisconsin

Sparta was then a community of about eight thousand. It is in western Wisconsin. It turns out that the Amtrak train that I took to and from medical school in Chicago went right through Sparta, but it didn't stop there, so I didn't recognize the town.

The medical community consisted of five family practitioners in the Sparta Clinic and two others in private practice. I would be the only surgeon in town. The hospital was affiliated with a larger organization in La Crosse and had forty beds, including medical-surgical, pediatric, and obstetrics. There were two operating rooms, a nurse anesthetist, and a special care unit. Surgical call coverage was available from a general surgeon in the next town, Tomah. I liked the location. I could attend CME (continuing medical education) in Chicago or Madison or at the Mayo Clinic or the University of Minnesota—all were within driving distance.

There had been a surgeon in town, but he had left in early December. There had been surgeons in Sparta for about ten years. Up until 1970, all surgery done in Sparta was done by the general practitioners. Then the Sparta Clinic decided to hire a surgeon. The first one lasted less than a year. The second was in Sparta for five years and then left to complete a year of residency so he would be board eligible. He was followed by another surgeon who was in Sparta for one-and-a-half years. The most recent surgeon had been in Sparta from January 1978 to December 1982, five years. So I would be the fifth general surgeon in town.

I started at the Sparta Clinic in January 1983. I was busy right away. I did 238 cases in 1983. Somewhere I had read that the average surgeon does about 150 cases a year. I took out forty gallbladders and fourteen appendixes. I did twenty-nine hernia repairs, twelve C-sections, twelve hysterectomies, twenty-two tubal ligations, eight ovarian surgeries, and seventeen D&Cs. I performed ten exploratory laparotomies, seven bowel resections, three gastric resections, and two gastrostomies. I did three mastectomies for breast cancer, one of which was on a male patient. I had not had any training in endoscopy in residency or in North Dakota, so I took colonoscopy and gastroscopy training in the summer and did thirty-two scoping procedures later that year.

We took care of a lot of trauma patients, including two gunshot wounds to the abdomen. For one case, I had to testify in court about where the track of the bullet went. Other trauma cases included car accident victims, several of whom had intra-abdominal bleeding that required a splenectomy. I took care of burn patients and mild head injuries. I did an omental patch on a perforated ulcer and treated patients for perforated diverticulitis. I drained perirectal abscesses and did hemorroidectomies and resected pilonidal cysts. I didn't do tonsillectomies or fix hip fractures.

One of the family practitioners did fixation of hip fractures on nonambulatory patients. I assisted on those cases. I placed the spinal anesthetic because the nurse anesthetist didn't do spinals. The anesthetist would monitor the patient once the spinal anesthetic was in. On one patient, only the side that we were going to work on went to sleep from the spinal. Perfect!

I administered chemotherapy in the clinic. The oncologist would see the patient and start the treatment in La Crosse, and then I would continue it closer to home. Some of those patients I would see every week for one or two years.

I had some memorable patients. One lady presented with a rectal cancer that I removed as a low anterior resection. I put the bowel back together with a circular stapling device because it was so far down in the pelvis I couldn't see to sew it with sutures, and I wanted to leave her rectal sphincter intact. She just recently passed away—thirty years later.

Another lady presented with a bowel obstruction due to colon cancer. We did a bowel resection and created a colostomy. Later I took the colostomy down and there was no evidence of any more cancer. She survived for many years. Usually if a patient has a cancer so big it obstructs the bowel, it has also spread elsewhere.

A third lady presented with a small bowel obstruction. On exploration, I discovered that she had a loop of small bowel stuck in a hole in the mesentery of one of her fallopian tubes. That is a very rare type of internal hernia. But in addition to that, she had no broad ligaments. Broad ligaments are the wide attachments that go from each side of the uterus to the sides of the pelvis. She didn't have any. I could pass my hand under the fallopian tube from front to back and back to front without encountering any tissue. It was a wide-open space. It wasn't supposed to be like that. She had apparently gotten along fine that way. She'd had children with no problem. I considered writing an article about her hernia and absence of broad ligaments but never got around to it. I did do a literature search and could find only one article published on that particular type of internal hernia, nothing on the absence of broad ligaments.

One of the family practitioners had practiced in Sparta for many years and knew his patients' families well. Whenever he referred a patient to me, he would give me the entire family history as well as the medical history. He also liked to joke a bit. He was known to walk around the clinic with a rectal thermometer in his pocket.

When he was asked about it or when he reached for a pen and found the thermometer instead he would say, "Some asshole's got my pen!"

One day he referred an elderly hospitalized patient to me for surgery. While I was in the room explaining to the patient what we needed to do, the family practitioner was out in the hall with the family. They were concerned about my ability as a surgeon because they apparently thought I looked too young. They asked, "Where did she do her surgical training?" He told them, "St. Paul Ramsey Medical Center in St. Paul, Minnesota." That didn't seem to satisfy them. They asked, "Where did she go to medical school?" He told them, "The University of Chicago Pritzker School of Medicine." They still didn't seem to be satisfied so they asked, "Where did she go to college?" He told them, "Augustana College in Sioux Falls, South Dakota." They said, "Oh, okay." They were apparently familiar with that school and were finally satisfied that I knew what I was doing. When he shared that story with me, I thought it was interesting that it wasn't my medical or surgical training that counted. What counted was what they were familiar with.

In 1984, I did 326 cases, and the numbers continued to climb. The peak was in 1989 with 374 cases. I was very busy, and I enjoyed what I was doing. Part of my enjoyment came from the fact that we had a good surgical crew. In a small rural hospital with only one operating room, you work closely with the same people every day. When I started in Sparta, the OR supervisor was Sister Mary Aquin. She only managed the OR at that time, but in her earlier years she had managed the OR, OB, the medical/surgical ward, and the ER, and she was also the hospital administrator, all at the same time. She remembered when they used to wash the gloves between cases. They had a lot more patients in the hospital then, and the fourth floor of the hospital was a dorm for the nursing students they were training. Sister Mary Aquin lived in a house across the street from the hospital with two other elderly nuns.

The scrub nurse was Jean Weidl. She had been working in the hospital since she was sixteen and had been a scrub nurse for twenty-eight years. When I first started in Sparta, I said to her, "Give me the instrument that I need, not necessarily the one I ask for." She had so much more experience than I did.

The other scrub nurse was a young lady named Kim. I remember that she had to sit out during one case we were doing because she was in early pregnancy and got nauseated. I was eight months pregnant at the time, and we were doing a C-section. Sister Mary Aquin had to scrub in to help me finish the case. That was the only time that happened.

The circulating nurse was Dorothy Lewiston. She was very competent and became a close friend. The nurse anesthetist was Mary Weber. She did her job very well. I don't remember a case in which we had a problem with anesthesia.

That was the entire surgery crew. All female.

One patient had a D&C and had to return for a hysterectomy. She shared, "What I remember about my D&C was that you were talking about a chocolate cake recipe when I fell asleep."

Since we were so limited in personnel, I would frequently help out. I would help transport the patient to the OR. I would sometimes put in the IV or urinary catheter. I would assist the anesthetist in putting the patient to sleep. If she couldn't get the patient intubated, I would do it. I put in all the spinal anesthetics. I would help move the patient to the cart after surgery and help transport the patient to the recovery room. This wasn't anything new actually. It was the way I did things. When I was a resident, the surgeons would spend their time between cases in the lounge smoking cigarettes and drinking coffee. I never did learn to drink coffee, and with my sinuses, I couldn't stand being in the room where they were smoking. So, I was always in the OR helping get the room and patient ready. Also, my mother had taught me to always clean up after myself, so I naturally picked things up and put them away. The OR crew always expressed their appreciation.

Initially, the family practice doctors would assist at major surgeries. Some of them were very comfortable in the OR, while others would prefer to be elsewhere. Once we started doing laparoscopic procedures, the OR personnel would assist, so there would be no other physician present during those cases. Eventually, it was very rare that the family practice doctors would assist. They preferred to be seeing patients in the clinic. The only cases they were there for were the C-sections. After the baby was delivered, the doctor would take the baby to the warmer and care for him or her there. The scrub nurse would help me close. Once we had more surgeons, we would occasionally help each other, but that was rare. I was on my own most of the time.

Outside the door of the OR is a plaque that is a prayer:

> Divine Healer of the sick, Christ Jesus our Lord
> Without whose aid we can do nothing,
> Look down with favor upon us about to perform this operation
> And direct our minds and our hands
> That our work may be praiseworthy unto thee
> And successful unto those who suffer.
> In all things thy will be done. Amen.
> St. Luke, Patron of Physicians, pray for us.

I would see this prayer every morning as I was going into the OR. It gave me pause and put things in perspective.

My patients were cared for on the med-surg floor. We had a very good group of nurses. We did not have an ICU, but we did have a special care unit with cardiac monitoring and one-on-one nursing. We had respiratory therapy and a ventilator. We didn't use the ventilator very often. I screened the patients I would operate on, and if they had significant cardiac or respiratory disease, I would transfer them to La Crosse for their surgery because they had the resources to better care for them there.

I could be choosy about which cases I did because La Crosse was so close—thirty minutes away. We did what we could, but we recognized our limitations. The thing that a small rural hospital can offer that a larger institution can't is personal attention from people you know. I believe it is best to do a few select things very well rather than try to do everything. What we did, we did well.

8

Credentials and Teaching

All physicians are required to obtain a medical license from the state medical examining board before they can practice in a particular state. In 1982, I had a license in Minnesota and North Dakota. I had to apply for a Wisconsin license before I could start to practice in Sparta. Recently, I contacted the Wisconsin Medical Examining Board, and according to their records, I believe I was the second female general surgeon to be licensed in the state.

As I said earlier, you have to be invited by the American Board of Surgery to take the board exams. I took the written exam in Chicago in the fall of 1981. I passed and was invited to take the oral exams in San Diego when I was in North Dakota. They arrange to have you take the oral exams in a part of the country other than where you trained. Making arrangements to get to San Diego from Devil's Lake, North Dakota, proved to be a challenge. We rented a small plane to fly us to Bismarck and flew to California from there. A few days before we went to California, my husband was in a car accident. He wasn't injured badly, but the car was totaled, and it shook me up quite a bit. I use that excuse to explain why I failed to pass the oral boards the first time.

I was invited to retake the oral boards in March of 1983, soon after I came to Sparta. I was to take them in Denver this time. I was surprised to meet, in Denver, one of the surgeons who had just started practice in La Crosse. He was taking the exam also.

The exam was held in a hotel at the airport. The examiners sat at a small table in a hotel room, and I was to sit in a chair facing them. Just to my right was the bed. The exam consists of three sessions with two examiners each, and between sessions we stood in the hall waiting our turn. It didn't seem to be an appropriate venue. In response to one question, I couldn't remember the different types of testicular cancer. The examiner was trying to help me and asked what kind I would prefer my husband to have if he had it. Then he said, "Assuming you want him to stay around a while." It deteriorated from there. He said, "I bet if I had asked you about the types of ovarian cancer, you probably would have known all of the answers." Was that a sexist statement? I remember wishing I could just lie down on the bed and take a nap. However, I passed the exam! I was board certified! The certification was good for ten years. I didn't have to take the exam again until 1993.

Since you can have three tries to pass the exam, the American Board of Surgery invites you to take the recertification exam three years before your certification expires. The recertification exam is a written exam only. I took the recertification exam in 1991 and passed. I was good until 2003. I again took the recertification exam in 2000 and passed. I then was board certified until 2013. I didn't plan on taking the exam again because I would be retired.

To become a Fellow of the American College of Surgeons, you have to be board certified *and* to have practiced in one location for at least three years. I applied to become a Fellow in 1986. I had to list all the procedures I had done over the previous three-year period. Part of the application process was an interview before a panel of Fellows. I don't remember what questions I was asked, but I do remember that I was seven months pregnant at the time, and I remember thinking that they probably didn't have many applicants present in that condition. I became a Fellow of the American College of Surgeons in the fall of 1986. I didn't go to the ceremony at the annual meeting where the new Fellows are recognized because the meeting was in New Orleans that year, and I had a new baby to take care of. They sent me my certificate. Now I could put FACS after my name (Fellow of the American College of Surgeons).

I became a member of the Wisconsin Surgical Society in 1991. Initially, it was separate from the Wisconsin Chapter of the American College of Surgeons, but they frequently held joint educational meetings. Now they are merged. The Wisconsin Surgical Society meetings are very good. There are many presentations by students and residents. Members can give presentations also. I did a presentation about my trip to China in 1994. I did another in 2010 on how I did carpal tunnel releases under local anesthesia in the clinic (see chapter 18).

I had an opportunity to do some teaching soon after I came to Sparta. Physician assistant students from the University of Wisconsin in Madison were coming to Sparta to do a rotation with one of the family practitioners. The family practitioner asked me if I could share some interesting surgical cases with them. That developed into my being appointed as a surgical preceptor for the University of Wisconsin Physician Assistant Program in Madison. Students would spend six to eight weeks following me around, seeing patients, scrubbing for surgery, and taking call with me. Over the ten years from 1985 to 1994, twenty University of Wisconsin physician assistant students did surgical rotations in Sparta. I enjoyed spending time with them, and they were very good students. I learned a lot from them, and they challenged me to keep abreast of what was happening in surgery.

As a member of the hospital medical staff, I was required to be certified in advanced cardiac life support (ACLS). To maintain your certification, you have to take the course every two years. I found that it was difficult to remember the material in between courses because I didn't use it on a daily basis. And since I was a surgeon, I didn't get to use the skills very often because I didn't take care of cardiac patients or work in the ER. I had to do a lot of studying each time I needed to take the course. I learned that if I became an instructor in ACLS and helped teach the course twice a year, I wouldn't have to take the course. Also, I would be forced to review the material at least twice a year in order to teach it. That would help me remember it if I ever needed to use it in the clinic, hospital, or operating room. I took the instructor course and became an instructor of ACLS. Besides helping teach the courses in La Crosse on a regular basis, I developed review courses for the nurses at the Sparta Hospital to help them prepare for their recertification. In the early years, I know people didn't look forward to taking the course because it seemed to be so judgmental. They really came down on you hard if you didn't know an answer. More recently, ACLS is more interested in people learning the material and skills so they can help in a crisis situation than in whether they can pass a test. That has made it much more fun teaching the course.

Physicians may also be required to be certified in advanced trauma life support (ATLS). I liked taking care of trauma patients, and I initially took the ATLS course to make sure I was doing everything I could for them. I discovered that the material was very similar to the booklet I had put together as a resident on how to manage a trauma patient in room 10. I knew this stuff! Maintaining certification requires taking a recertification course every four years. Instead, I became an instructor in ATLS. If I taught at least one course a year, I didn't have to take the recertification course. I did have to retake the test if new material had been introduced, but I didn't have to study that hard because I kept up on this information and used it almost every day. Teaching ATLS to all the personnel who are involved in caring for trauma patients helps them treat patients faster and better, and I enjoy teaching it. The consistent sequence of care, which starts with identifying and treating life-threatening injuries first, helps keep us focused. For instance, you are not to be distracted by the very obvious leg bone sticking out of the skin at an odd angle when the patient is having trouble breathing.

9

Clinic Business

I was elected president of the Sparta Clinic in 1984 after I had been with the clinic only one year. I don't know what they were thinking! Initially there wasn't much to it. We had a clinic administrator who managed all the employees. We had people who did the scheduling and nurses who helped us care for the patients. We had people who did the paperwork and others who did the billing. We had cleaning people and someone to mow the lawn and shovel the snow.

And then we hired a new administrator. Things seemed to be going along fine until one day the pharmacist who rented space in our clinic brought to our attention the fact that a processed rent check he had written had been deposited at an institution where he didn't think we had an account. We checked it out and discovered that the new administrator had opened an account and had been embezzling money from us from almost day one.

We fired him and watched as he moved out of the office to make sure he didn't take anything that didn't belong to him. We looked in the desk and found paperwork that hadn't been taken care of that was months overdue. He had just stuffed things in drawers. So another one of the physicians and I took boxes of papers home and began sorting. I remember it was the spring of 1986. I was pregnant, and my husband was on a fishing trip. We eventually got all the paperwork back in order. We filed charges against the administrator, and he was jailed. He was fined, but we got back only a small portion of the money he had taken from us. A couple of years later, I got a request from him for a reference. Can you believe that?

I learned a lot about the paperwork involved in running a clinic that year. I signed the paychecks and paid the bills. The heads of departments stepped up to the plate and managed their people. I only had to fire one employee that I remember. I was involved in interviewing and hiring others. We survived. We looked for another administrator, and two years later we found a very good one. She became a personal friend and part of my support system when I went through my divorce. One of the hardest things I had to do as the president of the clinic was to ask a physician to leave. We thought it would be best if that physician worked someplace else.

In the late 1980s, the Sparta Clinic experienced quite a bit of physician turnover, and we became shortstaffed. The hospital also suffered because with fewer physicians there are fewer admissions to the hospital. FSH (Franciscan Skemp Healthcare), who owned the hospital, decided to start its own clinic in Sparta to recruit more physicians and thus keep the hospital open. It seemed to us that they thought that physicians were leaving because of us. At the same time, they wanted us at the Sparta Clinic to guarantee that we wouldn't affiliate with any other clinic. We couldn't do that. We didn't know what the situation would be like in the future. They initially used space in the hospital for the clinic. Two of our remaining physicians moved over to their clinic. That left us with only three physicians.

They soon outgrew their space in the hospital and wanted to build a clinic attached to the hospital. There was no space around the hospital unless they could close a block of Main Street and build there. The plan was to bring their proposal to the city council for approval. As president of the Sparta Clinic, I told them I was willing to say a few words in support of the proposal. I figured if that was what we needed to do to get more physicians to come and stay in Sparta, that's what we needed to do. As a surgeon, I needed more family physicians working in the area to refer surgical patients, and I needed the hospital because that was where I did surgery.

On the evening of the presentation to the city council, everyone met at the hospital to go over to City Hall together. It was at that point that the FSH leaders handed me a "script" of what they wanted me to say at the meeting. I couldn't believe it! They apparently didn't trust what I would say on my own and hadn't discussed it with me before then. I told them that while I was willing to speak in their favor, I wasn't willing to say what they had written. So I went with them and said, "If this is what we need to do to attract more physicians to come and stay in Sparta, then this is what we need to do." I wasn't convinced this was going to fix the problem.

The city council okayed the proposal, and they closed a block of Main Street and built a new clinic. As it turned out, they had physician turnover as well. Eventually, both clinics were able to recruit enough physicians to meet the needs of the community (in spite of the fact that the same "problem" physicians were at the Sparta Clinic). The fact that there were now physicians from two different clinics staffing the hospital raised a whole new set of challenges. I'll discuss them in the chapter on hospital politics.

In the early '90s, it became evident to us, the physician owners of the Sparta Clinic, that the business side of running the clinic was becoming burdensome. We couldn't keep up with all the regulatory changes and government requirements. We decided to explore the possibility of affiliating with a larger organization. We contacted the larger clinics in our area to see if anyone was interested in acquiring our clinic. The only response we got was from the Gundersen Lutheran Health System in La Crosse. We began negotiations and eventually got an offer from them to buy the clinic and the partnership.

The hospital in Sparta was owned and operated by Franciscan Skemp Healthcare, the other large medical entity in La Crosse.

Being that we were a clinic in Sparta, we thought it would be better for the community if we were affiliated with the same organization that ran the hospital. So before we signed any agreement with Gundersen Lutheran, we decided to contact Franciscan Skemp to see if they were sure they weren't interested in acquiring our clinic. They were, it seemed, suddenly interested. We met with the leaders of Franciscan Skemp Healthcare and told them what we needed. After that meeting, it happened that I got into an elevator with the CEO and the CFO of Franciscan Skemp. After the door closed, they asked me if it would be possible for me to give them a copy of the offer we had gotten from Gundersen Lutheran. I can understand why they asked, but I didn't think that was appropriate. We had just spent two hours telling them what we would need, essentially what Gundersen Lutheran had offered us. That sealed the deal for me. I needed to be able to trust the group I would be working with to do the right thing, and I didn't trust the leaders of Franciscan Skemp.

In July 1992, Sparta Clinic became part of the Gundersen Lutheran Health System. Our clinic administrator was given a position to manage several outlying clinics for the system, including ours, and I became the medical director of the Gundersen Lutheran Sparta Clinic. I found the Gundersen Lutheran Health System to be very good to work with. My experience with Franciscan Skemp had been that decisions were made in La Crosse as to how things were going to be done in their system and then were forced into implementation in Sparta. The Gundersen Lutheran System's response when I found myself in a difficult situation was, "You live in the community, Judy, and we trust your judgment. You do what you think best, and we will back you up." They recognized that the needs of a small community medical practice are not the same as those of a larger community.

I remained the medical director of the Gundersen Lutheran Sparta Clinic for ten years. I discovered that I liked administration. The clinic employees made it easy to be the leader. They very capably handled the day-to-day functioning of the clinic. When we affiliated with Gundersen Lutheran, some of the clinic activities/jobs were transferred to La Crosse. But there are some things that have to be taken care of locally, so a good core group of employees stayed with the clinic in Sparta. What I miss most about being retired is the people I worked with at the clinic.

10

Marriage and Motherhood

I met my first husband just before I started my internship. One day, after finding a place for me to live in St. Paul, my parents and I attended a company picnic for the insurance company my father worked for. My future husband was apparently working for the same company and was at the picnic. My mother was very proud of the fact that her daughter was a doctor, so when I was introduced to anyone, she said, "She's a doctor." My future husband caught her up short by asking, "What kind of doctor?" To my mom, there was only one kind of doctor.

We dated during my internship year. I liked the fact that he was tall and broad shouldered. He was very metropolitan, and I was not. We were married during my week off between internship and residency. In retrospect, marrying him was not the best decision. There were red flags, but I chose to ignore them. Despite what I had accomplished, I had a low opinion of myself. I fell hard for the first American male who showed an interest in me. I was ready to be loved.

My first husband and I were married for eleven years. During that time, he tried his hand at several different kinds of jobs, none for very long. He had had back surgery and frequently complained of back pain. This supposedly limited the kind of work he could do. When I met him, he was on workers' compensation. During my residency, he worked for the highway department, got a real estate license, and started a dog kennel. When we moved to North Dakota, he listed his occupation as a writer. It must have been hard to be known as the doctor's husband.

In Sparta he helped in a flooring business and a heating business. But mostly, he didn't work.

He treated his back pain with prescription medications and traction. We went through some difficult times. We got some counseling. Thinking things were going to improve, we decided to have a baby.

I planned my pregnancy around my schedule. I reviewed my caseload over the previous two years, and it appeared that the number of surgeries I did in May was lower than in other months, so I aimed for the first of May. I knew I would have to have two surgeons cover for me, because none of the general surgeons in La Crosse did C-sections. I would have to have a general surgeon and an obstetrician cover my practice.

I felt good during my pregnancy! I had a little morning sickness, but I found that if I ate a couple of soda crackers before getting out of bed and didn't eat breakfast until later, I did okay. I would go to the hospital and do my first case and then the whole OR crew would go to the cafeteria with me for breakfast.

I was able to do my prenatal physician visits in Sparta until late in the pregnancy. Then I started going to La Crosse. I figured I would deliver in La Crosse because I was the only one in Sparta who could do a C-section if that was needed. I remember the tour of the delivery room. I didn't tell them I was a physician because I wanted them to tell me everything. I didn't know much about having a baby, and I feared that if they knew I was a physician they would assume I knew a lot. I told them at the end of the tour what kind of work I did.

I worked until the day I was due. I remembered one of the surgeons from my residency had a large ventral abdominal hernia and could reach the OR table with his big abdominal bulge, so I didn't think my condition would be any different.

I was due April 30 and had arranged for surgical coverage for the following seven weeks. After April 28, I sat at home waiting for labor to start. Nothing happened for two weeks. My OB doc and I decided to induce labor. I couldn't afford to lose any more of my surgical coverage. I went to the hospital on Monday morning, and he ruptured the membranes. Then they gave me an enema, and things started happening. The nurse checked me at one o'clock and I hadn't progressed much, so the doc asked, "Do you want to start pitocin?" I said, "Yes, let's get this done." Pit was started, and the contractions got stronger. I think I did well with the Lamaze breathing. I had my spot on the wall to look at when I lay on my left side, and I had the fetal monitor to look at when I lay on my right side. At about 5 p.m., my body suddenly pushed. I was amazed. Through no conscious effort of my own, my body pushed. The nurse examined me and found I was ready. She called the doctor and told me not to push. How do you do that when your body does it on its own?

The doctor was able to finish his clinic before he was called. I was so accommodating. When he arrived and got ready, he said I could push, and with one big push my son was born. I apparently tore the cervix when I pushed, so that had to be repaired along with the episiotomy. While he was sewing me up, the doc asked, "Is there anything you need?" I said, "I'm hungry." They got me something to eat. When I got to my room, I called my parents and said, "I did it!"

I recovered rapidly, but I really wasn't ready to go back to work when my coverage ran out after five weeks. I was trying to breastfeed, so I didn't get much sleep. I remember one day fighting to stay awake as I was seeing a patient in an exam room. Luckily, my son, Matt, began sleeping through the night very early on, so I could function better during the day. I found I wasn't able to meet Matt's needs with breastfeeding, so we soon advanced to bottle feeding. I was and am still amazed that God would trust me with the care of a child.

It's the most important job you ever have, and you don't have any training for it.

My husband said he would take care of our son while I was at work. One day I came home for lunch at noon and found Matt sitting in the high chair entertaining himself while my husband was asleep in the chair in front of him. One evening, I was called to the hospital for an emergency. My husband said he would watch Matt, but when I got home the house was dark, Matt was under an end table screaming, and my husband was asleep in his recliner. After that, I took Matt to a daycare. I didn't trust my husband to put Matt's needs ahead of his own.

I began assessing the situation. I could see how my husband's behavior was affecting my son, but I had been unaware of how his behavior had been affecting me. I now realized that we always did what he wanted to do. We socialized with his friends. I had become estranged from my family. He picked out what clothes I would wear or how I would wear my hair. I was becoming someone I didn't like. I couldn't understand how I could be such a success at work and such a failure at home. It seemed as if I couldn't do anything right. I realized that I would come home and make an assessment of what mood my husband was in and then decide what mood I should be in. It was like walking on egg shells. I never knew what to do or feel. I began going to a counselor. I wanted to fix things. I didn't want a divorce. I was committed and believed in my marriage vows.

In the spring of 1987, when our son was eleven months old, I decided I needed to get away for a while. I rented and moved into a small house in town. I continued to pay the mortgage on our house, and my husband continued to live there. Matt went to daycare during the day, and if I was called to the hospital during the night or on weekends, I would take Matt with me, and the nurses would watch him while I worked.

In August 1987, I accepted Jesus as my Lord and Savior, and I thought that was going to save my marriage. I moved back home. Within a short period of time, it became obvious to me that things hadn't changed. Things got worse and worse. In January, I filed for divorce.

I had read the book *Love Must Be Tough* by James Dobson. I confronted my husband. I said to him, "I can't live like this any more. You have to leave." And he did. This time, I was going to stay in the house.

After some counseling, he wanted to reconcile, but I needed to see some change before I was willing to do that. I watched and waited. I think that he had learned to talk the talk, but his behavior hadn't changed. I pursued the divorce. Matt was two years old.

Our divorce hearing was on October 31, 1988, in Viroqua. After two days of hearing, the judge granted the divorce. The settlement was that we would sell the Corvette, golf cart, bass boat and trailer, and motorcycle. All the proceeds from those sales would go to my husband. I got to keep my interest in the clinic and my retirement funds. We were granted joint custody, but I had primary placement. Visitation was to be every other weekend from Friday afternoon to Sunday afternoon and Tuesday evenings.

Going through the divorce was one of the hardest things I have ever done. I didn't trust my ex-husband, but now I had to allow Matt, a small child, to visit him every other weekend alone. The only way I could do it was to picture Matt in Jesus's lap when he was at his dad's house. I believed Jesus could take care of him better than I could.

Throughout the divorce process, several good friends became my support group. I learned that you can't get through a tough situation like that without strong support. I continued counseling for another year. It was a safe place for me to go to talk to someone, and the counselor kept telling me I was okay. I needed to hear that. For eleven years, my husband had been telling me I was the one with the problem. I think we both had problems.

After the divorce, Matt spent his days at a very good daycare. They were very accommodating of my schedule. I also made arrangements with a neighbor girl, so if I was called in at night, she would come over and sleep at my house so I wouldn't have to wake Matt. He/we did okay.

In the summer of 1990, a friend of mine showed me an article in the La Crosse paper about how a man was suing a motorcycle group for beating him up at gunpoint and throwing him down his basement stairs. That man was my ex-husband. This had apparently happened a year earlier in 1989. I immediately checked to see if Matt had been there at the time of the alleged incident. He hadn't, but I stopped visitation at that point because if those kinds of things were happening at my ex-husband's house, I didn't want Matt going there. My ex-husband filed a contempt of court charge against me. The sheriff delivered the legal papers to me in the lobby of the clinic.

The hearing for this charge was on October 31, 1990. After four hours of hearing, the judge said, "In order for me to find her in contempt, she would have had to withhold visitation for no good reason. I think she had a good reason, so I do not find her in contempt." My ex-husband asked, "What about visitation?" The judge replied, "You didn't ask me to rule on visitation. All you did was file a contempt-of-court charge." The judge assigned the responsibility of writing up the findings of the hearing to my attorney. When she wrote the document, she included a statement that visitation would now be every other Saturday from 10 a.m. to 4 p.m. The judge signed the document. Matt never stayed overnight at his dad's again until he was eighteen years old.

When Matt was about six years old, he got a cut on his forehead. He and some other small boys were playing "King of the Hill" on a pile of dirt at church. He was pushed off and fell on a bicycle, which caused the cut. I took him to the ER and numbed up the area and sewed up the laceration. He was a real trooper. Several weeks later, I got a bill. So I did the work, and then I got the bill. I guess the paperwork has to go through all the proper channels.

When Matt was twelve years old, he spent his weekdays at an activity center during the summer months. One day the activity center called and told me Matt had vomited while they were at the pool and was now sleeping, which he didn't do normally. They wanted me to know what was happening, but since he was sleeping, we decided to leave him there until I picked him up after work. When I picked him up, he didn't want to walk to the car. He wanted to be carried. I couldn't carry him anymore. He was too big. He crawled into the car and lay down. When we got home, he went into his bedroom and lay down again. This certainly wasn't his normal behavior. I asked him, "Where do you hurt?" He said, "In my stomach." I had him lie on his back and examined him and thought he was tender on the right side. The clinic had already closed, but I called one of the lab techs and asked her if she would meet me at the clinic to do a blood count. She did, and his white blood count was elevated. I waited until my husband (this was my second husband) got home and told him that I thought Matt might have appendicitis. He said, "Well does he or doesn't he?" I said, "I'm the mother, not the doctor."

We took Matt to the ER in La Crosse because I wasn't comfortable operating on my own family. Matt slept on the cot in the ER until the surgeon came in. Then he sat up and looked as if nothing was wrong. Oh, boy! That didn't look good for me.

The surgeon asked Matt, "When did your stomach start hurting?" He said, "This morning." He hadn't said anything to me! Then the surgeon asked him, "Where did the pain start?" Matt said, "All over." "Where is the pain now?" Matt said, "In the right lower quadrant." Who other than a surgeon's son would answer that way? It was determined that he did have appendicitis, and they took out his appendix later that night.

The next morning, while the nurse and I were completing the paperwork, Matt started getting out of bed. I asked him, "Where are you going?" He said, "I want to see where I am." The nurse asked, "Should I give him some pain medication?" I told her, "If he's getting up on his own, he apparently doesn't need it." He went home the next day.

Matt and I have a very close relationship. He did rounds with me when he was small. The patients liked to see him. He seems to understand the time commitment surgery requires. I have tried very hard to be there for him.

We went on the safety patrol trip to Washington, DC, when he was in fifth grade. I was also able to go as a chaperone on his senior class trip to New Orleans. It was a last-minute opportunity, but I asked the patients I had scheduled for surgery to reschedule so I could do it, and they were all very willing. We made it work.

With counseling and advice from godly friends, I healed after my divorce. My self-esteem improved. I learned that reason must be involved in selecting a spouse, not just emotion. I got to the point where I was comfortable with who I was and realized I didn't need to be married. Then God gave me my second husband. I always liked to read Christian romance novels as an escape, and my first husband criticized me about it and said things never happened the way they did in books. Well, I proved him wrong. My second husband and I were taken with each other right away. We met on a blind date. I immediately liked his smile, his broad shoulders, and his teasing ways. We talked on the phone a lot over the next three weeks. On the second date, he took me to meet his parents. We were married a year later. He is a cranberry farmer, so he understands what being on call means.

When I remarried, I became a stepmom to two grown boys and a step-grandmother to a little girl. Now, twenty-three years later, that little girl and another granddaughter have grown up and married and have daughters of their own, our great grandchildren. We also have two other young grandchildren. We are truly blessed. God is a God of second chances.

11
Faith

I was raised Lutheran, and our family was very active in the church. We attended church services and Sunday school every Sunday. We participated in Vacation Bible School, and my parents were active in leadership. The two families we most socialized with were in the same church. One summer, our family attended Bible camp. I attended confirmation classes and was confirmed at the age of twelve. When I was a senior in high school, I was the Sunday school superintendent. I learned a lot about God and Jesus and Christianity. I knew the creeds and words. I accepted it all because it was what my parents believed.

I went to a Lutheran college, but I didn't go to church there. I was required to take a religion class, but I didn't do very well in it. I didn't understand what all the fuss was about. I drifted further away from my parents' beliefs while I was in medical school and residency. I saw no benefit to faith or church.

During residency, I learned that one of the authors of the primary text for heart disease was a cardiology fellow who had fudged data in the research he used to support what he wrote in the book. I remember thinking, "I can't even trust what I read in the medical books and journals. Where do I find the truth?"

I was married the first time in a Lutheran church, but my husband and I never attended church or did anything religious. My husband called himself a Pentecostal and was always quoting Scripture to me.

When our son was born, my husband and I agreed that we wanted him dedicated in a church. Knowing my husband would find something wrong with any church I chose, I told him to choose the church. He picked out Faith Evangelical Free Church in Sparta and called the pastor. The pastor was new at the church and was excited about doing the baby dedication. We then found out he lived across an empty lot from us and was also expecting a baby. We had the baby dedication, but we still didn't start going to church.

In 1987, the summer I separated from my husband, I started attending Faith Evangelical Free Church regularly and began Bible study. I learned that Christianity is a relationship. You can't get to heaven on your parents' beliefs. You have to choose for yourself. I had learned all about God and Jesus, but I had never heard that I needed a personal relationship with Jesus. I began to read the Bible on my own. The pastor gave me a copy of C. S. Lewis's *Mere Christianity*, which presents a reasoned argument for faith in Christ. As a scientist, I needed to know the reason behind the belief. It all made sense. It was the truth. I could depend on it. In August 1987, I accepted Christ's gift of salvation and was baptized. I had found the *truth*.

I am a sinner, and the wages of sin is death. Through no work of my own can I gain entrance to heaven or be saved. Only through faith in Jesus Christ as the Son of God who came to earth as a baby, was crucified, and rose again could I be saved. Salvation is a gift, freely offered. All I had to do was accept it. Jesus is the way, the truth, and the life. In response to what Jesus has done for me, I want to do what is pleasing to him. I learn about him and find out what pleases him by reading the Bible.

I continued to grow as a Christian. When my husband would tell me what the Bible said about something, I would ask him where it said that, and he would not be able to tell me. I believed what the Bible said was true, and I searched for answers in it. I applied what I learned. God began shaping me into who he wanted me to be, more like Christ.

I studied what God said about marriage and divorce. I took my marriage vows seriously. I didn't want a divorce. But the reality was that being married to my husband was killing me; it had changed me into someone I didn't know and I didn't like.

I really struggled with filing for divorce because I wanted to do the right thing, and what I was doing wasn't specifically listed in the Bible as a legitimate reason for divorce. I sought counsel from wise and godly people. I finally decided that I had to do it for myself and for my son. I also did it for my husband. I hoped it would shock him into realizing that what he was doing wasn't good.

I got support from the pastors and members of the church as I went through the divorce. I attended small group Bible studies and grew as a Christian. Some of the people in those groups became my closest friends. I began to blossom. I discovered that if your home life is stable, you can do more outside the home.

I became a deaconess at church. I sang in the choir and on the worship team. I helped set up the library. I currently teach adult Sunday school classes and serve on committees. I am involved in decorating the church and tending the gardens. When you realize what Jesus has done for you, you can't help but want to give back.

Before becoming a true believer, I was a surgeon who called herself a Christian. After giving my life to Christ, I was a Christian who happened to be a surgeon. It changed everything, especially my priorities. My most important relationship is with Christ. My second priority is my relationship with my husband, followed by my relationship with my child. My job as a surgeon is in fourth place. Being a child of God defines who I am. I do believe that God is in control and has been in control throughout my life, even though I didn't always recognize it. In retrospect, I can see that the way everything came together for me to become a surgeon had been directed by God. I believe being a surgeon is a calling from God, and the way in which I practice my calling is to glorify him.

I attended a course called "The Saline Solution" to learn how to share my faith with my patients in the short time I have with them in the clinic and hospital. As Christians, we are called to be salt in the world, and the most common solution we give patients is salt water or "saline," thus the name of the course. We learned how to raise faith flags (comments about faith during our interactions with patients) to allow patients the opportunity to ask questions or to share their own experiences. We learned that it is okay to ask the patient if we can pray with them and for them. Spirituality is an important part of all of us and it is okay to recognize it. This course changed the way I practiced surgery. I began to view every appointment as an appointment that God had made. I would ask myself before I walked into each exam room, "What is God doing in this person's life, and how can I best come alongside and help him?" Rather than reluctantly going into a room where I knew a patient could be a challenge, I saw each appointment as an opportunity. My attitude was the key.

I attended a lecture by the executive director of the Christian Medical and Dental Associations at one of their meetings. It was on what it means to be a Christian doctor. He said the first criterion is to be a competent physician. That initially surprised me. I thought he was going to say something about faith. But now it makes sense. I am Christ's representative here on earth. I want to draw others to him. The best way I can do that is to be good at what I do as a surgeon, using the gifts he has given me.

I wanted my son to attend a Christian school. There was one in La Crosse, but transportation would be a problem, and I wanted to be involved in the school my son attended. I couldn't go to La Crosse. It was out of my call range. God led me to become involved in starting a Christian school in Sparta. A local woman was burdened to start a Christian school and called a meeting inviting anyone in the community who might be interested. Out of that meeting, five people came together as a steering committee and started the process. I was one of them.

We worked for two years on the paperwork and were able to open the doors of Sparta Area Christian School to students in the fall of 1995. We started small, but God blessed us in amazing ways. He provided the facility, the teachers, the curriculum, the finances, and all the other needs. The school grew to a maximum of sixty students. Matt attended school there from fourth to tenth grade, and I was able to be very active in the school. God closed the doors of the school after eleven years of service. It was a great blessing to us and to the community.

The second year the school was open, a student attended the school who needed some help with reading. After a year in the Christian school, she went on to successfully complete her schooling at the public school. I am now on the board of directors of a ministry she started for homeless mothers.

I like the church I attend because the men are the leaders and they "walk the talk." The leaders seek God's leading in everything they do. The mission statement is, "Leading people in a fully devoted, life-changing relationship with Jesus Christ."

I see God at work in my life on a daily basis. He provides the most amazing opportunities and resources, and He continues to direct my life. In one very difficult situation as the president of the clinic, God gave me just the right words to say. He has directed my thoughts and hands during many procedures. I especially like a picture I have of a surgeon doing an operation. It's a painting by Nathan Greene called "Chief of the Medical Staff." It shows Jesus standing behind the surgeon and guiding his hand. He is the healer, and I am the instrument. He has blessed me with gifts and skills, and I honor him by using them.

I recently participated in a general surgery missions trip to Honduras sponsored by the Christian Medical Association and the Baptist Medical and Dental Mission International. We did many surgeries, but the best thing of all was that the entire OR crew prayed together with the patient before each procedure. God is great!

12
1993

1993 was a significant year in my life. In the spring, I attended The International Conference on Women's Health in China. In that year, I was also diagnosed with Grave's disease and had my thyroid irradiated. In July, I attended my first bioethics course. There was a common bile duct injury during a laparoscopic cholecystectomy I performed in August. In October, I began working with a steering committee to get a Christian school started in Sparta. And I did an emergency C-section for a patient with placenta abruption in November that resulted in a malpractice lawsuit. These were all life-changing events.

China

My trip to China actually began in December 1992. I received a written invitation in the mail from the Chinese Medical Association to attend The International Conference on Women's Health in Beijing. This wasn't a general mailing. It was in an envelope addressed to me personally. Why would the Chinese Medical Association be writing to me? I was intrigued, but I initially didn't take it seriously.

Over the Christmas holiday, my parents were visiting, and one day we invited a couple from Sparta, friends of my parents, over for coffee. They had just returned from China and told me that if I had an opportunity to go, I should take it. So I replied to the invitation and signed up to go.

Apparently the Chinese Medical Association had contacted the American Foundation for International Cooperation and Development in Seattle, Washington, and asked for their help in setting up this conference. They hoped to make it an annual event. The foundation handled the application and all travel arrangements. I paid for my own trip, and I went alone.

I flew from La Crosse to Chicago and from there was on standby to get on a flight to San Francisco. The flight arrangement worked out, so I got to San Francisco on time. At the hotel in San Francisco, I met my roommate and other members of the US delegation to the conference. The next morning, we flew from San Francisco to Tokyo, then to Shanghai, and then to Beijing; it was about twenty-two hours all together. We finally got to our hotel. It was the newest hotel and the tallest building in Beijing. I turned the TV on, and there were the same cartoons we watched at home.

The first four days of our visit was the conference. It was in the same hotel where we were staying. The purpose of the conference was to share information we could take back to the organizations we represented. I didn't know what organization I was representing.

The conference had a very full schedule. There were plenary sessions, panel discussions, and paper presentations. Some of the plenary speakers were the Vice President of the Chinese Medical Association, the Chair of the National Women's Health Network of China, the Minister of Health and the Environment for the Republic of Marshall Islands, the Director of the Department for Women Workers Labor Protection in the All-China Federation of Trade Unions, the Director of the Ministry of Health of Indonesia, and the President of the International Confederation of Midwives.

Other officials attending the conference included the Coordinator for nursing affairs of the Commonwealth Regional Health Secretariat for East, Central, and Southern Africa; the Director of the Latin American Center for Perinatology and Human Development; a representative of the World Health Organization; representatives of the Women's Global Network for Reproductive Rights; the Director of ALETTA; the President of the Inter-African Committee on Traditional Practices; the Chairman of the International Professional Union of Obstetricians and Gynecologists; the Secretary General of the Asia and Oceania Federation of Obstetricians and Gynecologists; and the Director of the Bureau of Women and AIDS of the Netherlands. The only representative of organized medicine from the US was the President of the American Medical Women's Association.

Panel discussions included "The Female Infant, Child, and Adolescent," "The Working Professional Woman," "The Sexually Active Woman," "Traditional and Non-Traditional Approaches to Healthcare," "The Aging Woman," and "The Pregnant Woman and Mother." The moderator for "The Aging Woman" was from Milwaukee, Wisconsin.

One could select from multiple paper presentations. Most of them were given by attendees from the US, as we had by far the greatest number of representatives—seventy. Apparently anyone could submit an abstract for a paper presentation. I attended several sessions, including one discussing the risk of infection from dental work in someone with a prolapsed mitral valve. The presenter was very angry that no one had told her of this risk and she had gotten an infection. Another was by a "victim" of breast cancer. Another was titled, "I'm Jewish."

My roommate was the director of women's health at Dallas Methodist Hospital. About the third day of the conference, I asked her if she considered the women in the US delegation to be representative of women in the United States. She said, "Oh no!

They are so far left, they are off the page." I said, "Thank goodness! I thought I had been out in the boonies too long."

After the conference, we took in the sights. In Beijing, we visited the Temple of Heaven and the Forbidden City and Palace Museum. The Forbidden City is where the emperor lived. It is very large. The throne is in the center of the Hall of Supreme Harmony, which is in the center of the Forbidden City, which is in the center of Beijing. The Forbidden City is surrounded by a moat and four walls with a gate in each. The large courtyard in front of the Hall of Supreme Harmony is all concrete and very thick so no one could tunnel in. The emperor had multiple bedrooms and would randomly choose which one to sleep in, so no one knew exactly where he was. These were just some of the precautions they took to protect him. All the buildings are made of wood and covered with colored tiles. Common themes are symmetry, dragons, lions, turtles, and herons. There are many large bronze pots full of water with places for fire beneath them to prevent the water from freezing. The water in these pots is used to put out fires. The pillars in the throne room are covered with gold.

We visited Tiananmen Square and Mao's tomb. We went to the Great Wall just outside Beijing. There is a wall around Beijing also. I didn't realize this was a common mode of defense outside of Europe.

We flew from Beijing to Xian on Chinese Air. Xian is the ancient capital of China and home of the Terra Cotta Warriors. We then went to Shanghai and did some shopping in an area that looks like London. They have a Big Ben and other similar architecture. We took the train to Suzhou. It is the Venice of the East. We visited the Grand Canal, the Master of Nets Garden, a silk-spinning factory, the Silk Embroidery Institute, and a jade-carving factory.

As we toured the country, we visited several hospitals. It is my understanding that the medical system in China is government run. Everyone has access free of charge. The lowest level of service is a village doctor. That would be someone like our nurse practitioner. Village doctors are responsible for clean water, sanitation, immunizations, birth control, perinatal care, blood-pressure screening, Pap smears, and the treatment of minor illnesses. What cannot be handled by the village doctor goes to the township or county facility. They have the capacity to deliver babies, do IV hydration and medications, perform C-sections, and minor surgeries, as well as to treat diabetes and high blood pressure.

Near Beijing, we visited the Shrenzi County Hospital. We toured the OR, which had the same basic equipment we do. We saw the OB ward. The newborns were in bassinettes at the foot of their mothers' beds. There was no heat in the hospital. This was early April. In the nurse's station, we were shown a chart rack with about six charts in it that was presented as "the records of all the pregnant women in the county." We don't know who all is pregnant in our town! Patients requiring more intensive care go to the provincial hospital, and so on up the line. The tertiary referral center is the Peking University Medical College and Women's Hospital in Beijing. It has all the high-tech equipment we have. It was built in 1921 with the help of the Rockefeller Foundation. We visited several of the ten-bed wards and the ICU. It also has a very large library.

The staff told us that everyone in China has access to every level of health care, but we observed that most people traveled by bicycle. So how does someone in outlying areas get to the university hospital?

We visited the Chinese Academy of Traditional Medicine in Beijing. Traditional Medicine in China is what we call alternative medicine or Chinese medicine. They demonstrated acupuncture and manipulation as treatment for stroke and sinus disease. The pharmacy had more than three thousand drawers of medicines and herbs. A typical prescription called for six or seven herbs, which were combined in little piles on a piece of paper. The paper was folded up and then could be boiled or steamed and the fluid taken orally or by IV. Alternatively, it could be made into a plaster and applied directly on an area.

In Xian we visited the Xian Medical College. Medical training in China can take one of three tracks. There is training in Western medicine, training in traditional medicine (which is what they did at the Xian Medical College), or a combination of both.

In Shanghai we visited the Shanghai Textile Hospital. They service about three hundred thousand workers, two-thirds of whom are women. They do some unique research there. They have a captive population, as workers seldom change jobs, and their employment requires a physical every other year. They shared how they had decreased the incidence of cervical cancer by treating cervical erosions with 5-fluorouracil and three herbs.

While I enjoyed the trip to China, I was overwhelmed and confused by the radical feminist agenda I was exposed to among the representatives from the United States. I never considered myself to be a radical or a feminist and didn't know much about it. It took me nearly a year to process my experience in China before I could talk about it. I eventually did a presentation at the Wisconsin Surgical Society Meeting about my trip.

To this day, I wonder why I got an invitation. Was it because I was a female surgeon? There were few of us in 1993. There was only one other female surgeon in the group from the United States, and she was from a small town also. There were a couple of ob-gyn docs, but most of the others were private citizens, nurses, or social workers. All were women. How did they choose?

I heard about a Fourth World Conference on Women's Health that was scheduled to be held in Beijing in 1995. It was moved out of Beijing because, apparently, it was so controversial. Hillary Clinton attended that one. I wonder if it was in any way related to the one I had attended.

Grave's Disease

In the spring of 1993, I noticed that my heart rate was faster than usual. My heart rate has always been slow. Normally, when I lay down at night, I could slow it even further by slowing down my breathing. One night I noticed it was going pretty fast for me, so

I tried to slow it down with my breathing. It didn't work. It just kept going fast. The next day I asked one of my colleagues about it, and he said it was probably due to stress. I asked another colleague, and he said there might be something wrong with my thyroid. We did a blood test, and I found out I was hyperthyroid. I looked up this condition in my medical books and discovered that I had been having other symptoms as well. I had weakness in my major leg muscles—I couldn't stand up from a squat in the garden. I had lost some weight (which was good). Another symptom was change in the thickness of my hair. When I read about these symptoms as a medical student I couldn't believe that a patient would complain of these things. I checked my hair and didn't notice any difference. Then it occurred to me that the change in the thickness of the hair would occur as it grew so the change wouldn't show up for two to three months.

After further testing, it was determined that I had an autoimmune disease of the thyroid called Grave's disease. The treatment was to slow down the thyroid. That could be done with medication to try to control the thyroid, or an alternative treatment was that the thyroid gland could be destroyed by radiation and then I would be on thyroid replacement for the rest of my life. I decided to take the radioactive iodine to obliterate the gland. It was taken as one dose orally, and for three days I couldn't be near my son to prevent exposing him to radiation.

No schedule was set up to periodically check my thyroid function to determine when the gland was no longer producing hormone and I would need to start taking replacement therapy. The doctor told me we would check my thyroid level when I developed symptoms of hypothyroidism. These symptoms included a slowing of metabolism, weight gain, a change in my hair that would only be evident later, tiredness, and a slowing of my heart rate. I didn't notice any of these symptoms.

One day in August, I did a routine laparoscopic cholecystectomy. The procedure went fine. I had videotaped it, as was my normal routine. Later that day, I was sitting in my office at the clinic, and I simply couldn't stay awake. I decided to check my thyroid function. We check the TSH or thyroid stimulating hormone, which is the hormone produced by the pituitary gland that tells the thyroid how much thyroid hormone to produce. If your thyroid is not making enough thyroid hormone, the TSH is high. Normally the TSH level is between three and five. Mine was eighty-five! I had never seen one that high. It meant my thyroid hormone level was very low.

Two days later, I recognized that the patient I had done the lap cholecystectomy on had a common bile duct injury that had apparently been caused by something I did during her surgery. I transferred her to La Crosse, and they were able to repair the injury. I have reviewed the tape of my procedure several times, and I cannot determine where or how an injury occurred. I wonder if I was so hypothyroid that I wasn't thinking straight during that procedure.

I started taking thyroid medication. The doctor told me it would take a year to get it regulated. I scoffed at him, thinking I could do it faster than that. It took a year!

Bioethics

In late May, I was paging through the spring quarterly publication of the EFCA (Evangelical Free Church of America), which I didn't normally do. My attention was drawn to an ad inside the back cover. It was promoting a summer course in bioethics that would kick off the bioethics degree program at Trinity International University in Deerfield, Illinois. The course was to be an intensive nine days of classroom lectures, and then we would be required to write two papers. It was actually two courses, one taught by Nigel Cameron, a bioethicist from Great Britain, and the other taught by O. J. Brown, a professor at Trinity. I had an interest in bioethics, but I had not had an opportunity to take any courses on it. It was a new field and had not been part of the curriculum of medical school when I was there. I felt compelled to take the courses. I wasn't sure I would be able to understand them since it was a lot of philosophy, and I was all science. I wasn't sure about being able to write a paper, either. But I felt as if I had no choice. I registered and prepared to go. I was able to stay with my sister and her family in a northern suburb of Chicago near Deerfield.

There were twelve people in both courses, and as we all introduced ourselves and explained why we were there, our stories all sounded the same. We all had felt compelled to be there. God at work! It was an amazing experience. I learned so much, and it sparked a deeper interest in bioethics that has continued to this day. I successfully completed the courses, I was able to write the papers, and I earned six credits toward a master's degree in bioethics.

Every summer since then, Trinity International University, along with the Christian Medical and Dental Associations, Nurses Christian Fellowship, Americans United for Life, the Center for Bioethics and Human Dignity, and other Christian organizations have sponsored a bioethics conference at Trinity. I have attended many. They have courses that surround the conference that you can take for academic credit. I have accumulated fifteen credits now. I am considering completing my master's in bioethics, but completing this book comes first.

It was at the first bioethics conference that I became aware of the Christian Medical Association. I became a member soon after that and have been truly blessed by that organization. They minister to and provide a support system for physicians through resources, books, and fellowship. They also represent Christian physicians in the public arena.

Christian School

In October of that very eventful year, I noticed an invitation in the local paper for anyone interested in starting a Christian school in Sparta to attend a meeting at the library. I attended the meeting and became part of the steering committee to put together a school. (The rest of the story is told in chapter 11.)

Finally, in November, I did a C-section that led to a lawsuit—I will tell you about this in the chapter on lawsuits.

13

Hospital Politics

As a physician/surgeon, I am employed by the clinic. In order to care for patients and do procedures in a hospital, I need to apply for privileges at the hospital. The application has to be approved by the existing medical staff and the board of directors of the hospital before I can do anything at their hospital. There are three categories of medical staff privileges depending on how involved I want to be in supervising the care of patients in the hospital. As a member of the active medical staff, I am actively involved in the care of patients in the hospital and am required to attend medical staff meetings and participate on committees. These are not requirements for consulting or courtesy staff.

I have had medical staff privileges at several hospitals. I started with active privileges at St. Mary's Hospital in Sparta and courtesy privileges at Tomah Memorial Hospital in Tomah, Hess Memorial Hospital in Mauston, Vernon Memorial Hospital in Viroqua, and St. Joseph's Hospital in Hillsboro. I eventually acquired active privileges at Tomah Memorial Hospital and added Black River Memorial hospital in Black River Falls and Tri-County Memorial Hospital in Whitehall to the courtesy list. Each hospital requires its own application forms be filled out. It's a lot of paperwork!

As the surgeon who did by far the most cases in the operating room in the Sparta hospital, I thought I knew best what kinds of surgeries we could do safely and what we did well. I found out that was not what others thought. In the mid 1990s, I was consulted on a patient needing an elective procedure. I didn't think that person was an appropriate surgical patient for the Sparta Hospital because of anesthesia concerns. Later, I found out that she was pregnant, and there was a good possibility that she would need an emergency C-section. I reminded the OB provider that I didn't think this patient was an appropriate surgical patient for our hospital in an elective situation. She was at a higher risk for a complication in an emergency situation, such as a C-section. C-sections under general anesthesia are a special situation. I am scrubbed, gowned, and ready to cut before the patient is put to sleep. I cannot help the nurse anesthetist if there are problems with the anesthesia. I thought voicing my concerns would influence their decision.

Apparently other arrangements for a possible C-section were made with a different surgeon and anesthetist so the patient could deliver in Sparta even though I thought she should go to La Crosse. Thankfully, when the patient presented in labor, it turned out the other surgeon wasn't available. The patient was transferred to La Crosse where she had a C-section. She did well.

It was after the fact that the OB provider told me about what had happened, because she didn't want me thinking they were doing anything behind my back. I don't understand how telling me about it later negated the fact that it was done without my knowledge.

A friend then informed me that the story around the hospital was that I didn't want to do this particular patient's surgery because I didn't like her. That hurt. I believe my decision to do a case is based on medical needs and what is best for the patient, not on personal feelings. I met with the hospital administrator, the head of nursing, and the OB provider to review the case and clear up misunderstandings. My impression of the meeting was they didn't understand what I was concerned about. So we moved on.

This incident led to me questioning what my role was and how much my opinion counted in the hospital. I was told I was not the chairperson of the department of surgery because we didn't have departments, so I couldn't make decisions as a department chair would. Apparently, I was just a surgeon who used the operating room.

When the Sparta Clinic became part of Gundersen Lutheran, the only things that changed from my perspective were that someone else signed my paycheck and I didn't have to make the business decisions anymore. My practice was exactly the same. I saw patients in the clinic and did surgery in the hospital. However, at the hospital, it felt like something significant had changed. I was treated differently.

As a surgeon, I need a hospital to do my work. I need an operating room, OR crew, recovery room, nursing unit, nurses, and support services, such as the lab, X-ray, and medical records. I work closely with all of these departments of the hospital. Once the FSH system started building its own clinic attached to the hospital (the clinic I worked for was across the street on the opposite side of the hospital), it seemed that all their time and energy went into that effort, and hospital work took second place. In my opinion, each hospital department was functioning independently with no oversight or accountability. Services suffered.

Initially I was told to fill out incident reports if variances occurred. I did that but never heard if the issue was addressed. Then the same thing would happen again, so I would fill out another incident report. Each individual incident wasn't life threatening, but over time I saw a pattern, and things were getting worse.

One day when I came back from a vacation, I discovered that there was a new person in charge of the OR. I was not informed that this was even being considered. I was not asked to participate in that person's selection or orientation. To my knowledge, she had not worked in an OR before, let alone been an OR supervisor. As more concerns arose, I suggested that maybe it would be appropriate for the nursing supervisor (who, in my opinion, knew nothing about the OR), the new OR supervisor, and I sit down and discuss the needs of the OR. That didn't happen. Each incident continued to be reported individually.

When it got to the point where I thought the situation was affecting patient care, I said, "No more!" The specific case involved a seventy-year-old female I had scheduled for a bowel resection for colon cancer. She was admitted to the hospital the night before surgery for her bowel prep. Lab work was ordered to be drawn on admission. I usually didn't lose much blood doing a bowel resection, but I always ordered a type and screen so we knew what blood type the patient was and could determine if we had blood available should we need it.

The next day, as we started the case, the anesthetist noticed a drop in the patient's blood pressure upon induction of anesthesia. We knew her hemoglobin was a little low at 10.0, which is common with colon cancer. She'd been functioning well at this level, but because of her age and her response to induction, I decided we should cross-match her blood and give her a couple of units before we lost any. It was at this point that the lab informed us that they didn't have her blood type available. We were already in the middle of the case! Why would I have ordered a type and screen unless I wanted to know that information before I started the procedure? When the lab did the type and screen and found that they didn't have any of her blood type available, they should have called me. I could have made arrangements to get her type of blood, decided to delay surgery, or determined that we would use universal type blood. (Usually you use universal type blood in emergency situations when you don't have time to do the cross match.)

We ended up using universal type blood, and the patient did fine. I did not want to find myself in that situation again. I decided not to do any more elective surgery at the Sparta hospital until issues were addressed. I gave notice in November of 1994. That sure shook things up!

An outside OR nurse was called in to evaluate how the hospital/OR functioned. One recommendation was to have weekly meetings between the nursing supervisor, the OR supervisor, the hospital administrator, myself, and a facilitator to address issues. Sound familiar? We reviewed each case for variances and looked at upcoming cases and what we would need. Those meetings were very productive.

As we reviewed cases, the facilitator noticed that we were only reviewing my cases. We were not reviewing the outreach surgeons' cases or the cases of the general surgeon who covered for me. I got the distinct impression that the hospital personnel thought I was the problem. The facilitator informed them that it was a hospital process problem, not a Dr. Lottmann problem. We continued our meetings addressing OR issues for several months. I resumed doing elective surgical cases in February 1995.

As part of their new clinic practice, FSH started a nurse midwife program. I knew what nurse midwives were, and I reviewed the protocols outlining how they would function in our community. I didn't have any concerns because I was familiar with how the physicians doing OB had functioned for years and assumed things wouldn't change since they would be overseeing the nurse midwives.

I have no training in OB. The OB physicians are in charge of the patient. If they decide a C-section is necessary, they call me and I do the procedure. Over the years I have acquired a good sense of when a C-section is indicated. The patient becomes my responsibility during their recovery from surgery.

Over the first couple of years of the midwife program, I began to notice that the OB patients we were caring for were more high risk than before. I was being asked to do C-sections on patients who had problems with which I was unfamiliar. I shared my observations and concerns. All the OB providers, the nursing supervisor, and I sat down and worked out what kind of OB patient was appropriate for our hospital.

J. LOTTMANN, MD

Medical School Graduation

ON CALL — *Hospital Politics*

Residency

Sparta Surgical Crew

Me Helping in the OR

Residency Reunion

ON CALL — *Hospital Politics*

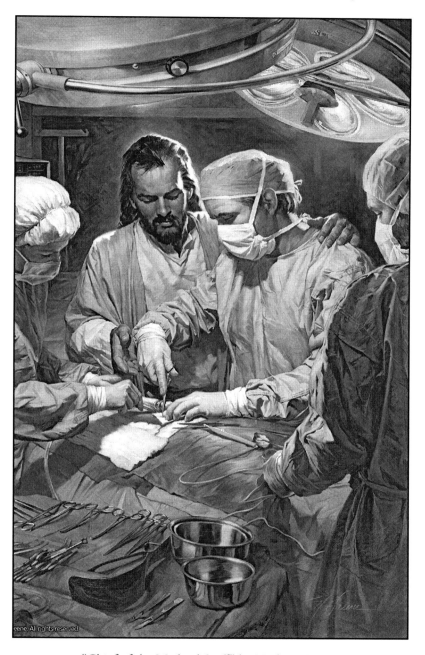

"Chief of the Medical Staff" by Nathan Greene

I believe we were tending to more high-risk patients because the two nurse midwives who had been hired had worked at larger institutions with obstetricians and were familiar with and comfortable caring for patients with more problems. The backup physicians in Sparta were interested in keeping as many patients as possible in Sparta and so were going along with the nurse midwives' decisions. For a while we were on the same page, but then I again began to see patients who I thought we had agreed were not appropriate for our hospital.

Finally, I was called in for a possible C-section on a patient with a breech presentation (the baby was coming butt first instead of head first). Once the breech presentation was confirmed by X-ray, the midwife wanted to try to deliver the baby vaginally. This was one of the situations we had decided was not appropriate in Sparta. The nurse midwife told me the patient had delivered vaginally before and had characteristics that were favorable for a vaginal delivery this time. It was my understanding that the backup physician had never done a breech delivery. I didn't think it was appropriate for the nurse midwife to be doing something the backup physician hadn't done and probably couldn't help her with if she got into a problem. Also, if she started a breech delivery and got stuck, there wasn't anything I could do to help. When I spoke to the OB providers about this concern, I was told they didn't need me to be making decisions about the OB practice in Sparta. All they needed me for was "my knife."

For me, this situation confirmed my conviction that something had to change. I believed they were putting patients and the hospital at risk. My practice was being put at risk as well. I needed to trust them to make the right decisions, and I found I *didn't* trust them anymore. I needed to be treated as a colleague and allowed to have input into the care of patients I was operating on.

I gave a two-week written notice to the hospital administrator that I was no longer willing to provide C-section coverage for the OB practice at the Sparta Hospital. The hospital was upset with me. The FSH system was very upset with me. They published a front-page article in the local newspaper about how I was refusing to do C-sections, which was causing them to shut down the OB practice in town. No one ever contacted me to hear my side of the story.

At the time, I was the medical staff president at the hospital. All the physicians took turns at this position, and it just happened that it was my turn. That had nothing to do with when I made my decision or why I made my decision. I showed up at the next medical staff meeting ready to conduct the regular meeting, and the FSH personnel were surprised I could do that. I explained to them that I was doing what I thought was best for the hospital. They didn't see it that way. They apparently thought my decision was Gundersen Lutheran trying to close the Sparta Hospital. Within a week they had recruited a locum tenens surgeon to do C-sections, and there was no loss of services.

In July 1995, FSH affiliated with the Mayo Clinic. They informed us that they would be hiring their own surgeon. They dissolved the local hospital board of directors so that the community had even less input into the hospital decisions. They combined the hospital and clinic into the Sparta Campus. Hospital committees became campus committees. As a member of the active medical staff of the hospital, I was required to serve on committees. I served on the Infection Control Committee and the Ethics Committee. Since these were now campus committees, I was being asked to make decisions that concerned their clinic. Also, the credentials of all providers on the campus had to be approved by the medical staff. As a member of the medical staff, I had no problem with those who had a hospital practice, but for me to approve the credentials for their clinic-only providers didn't seem right. We were, after all, competitors. We were the only facility in the FSH network where there were physicians on the medical staff who were not FSH physicians, and I don't think they knew how to deal with us.

In 1995, FSH began a GI (gastroenterology) outreach to Sparta. The GI physicians came to do endoscopy procedures. The scopes we originally purchased in 1983 had worn out, so every Thursday they brought their gastroscopes and colonoscopes with them to use. Then their GI department became short staffed, and they couldn't come to Sparta anymore. They continued to bring the scopes on Thursdays and designated their surgeon in Sparta as the one to use them to do the procedures.

I had patients I wanted to do colonoscopies on, so I asked if I, being a member of the hospital medical staff with the same privileges and credentials as their surgeon, could use the scopes. The answer was no. Apparently a Gundersen Lutheran surgeon couldn't be trusted to use FSH equipment. Yet, I was allowed to use their equipment in the OR every day on regular surgery cases.

Managed care presented a very interesting situation in Sparta. When Gundersen Lutheran developed a managed care product, the Sparta Hospital was not a provider for their network. A patient with Gundersen Lutheran managed care could not go to the local hospital for an X-ray, fluoroscopy, or a CT scan and have it paid for. I could do surgery on Gundersen Lutheran managed care patients in the hospital, but they would end up paying a large portion of the hospital charge themselves.

It got so ridiculous for a while that if a Gundersen Lutheran patient presented to the Sparta ER with appendicitis, I could do the surgery in Sparta, and it would be paid. But if the patient presented to the Gundersen Lutheran clinic, which was across the street, I'd have to send them to La Crosse for their surgery to be paid. Thankfully, both entities are more accommodating now.

In July 1996, FSH hired a surgeon for their clinics in Sparta and Tomah. My surgical case load dropped by two thirds. I had to decide if I wanted to stay in Sparta or go elsewhere. My credentials were good, so I could go anywhere, but my husband's parents lived here, and my son visited his father every other weekend in La Crosse, so I was essentially tethered. I decided to stay. I liked the people I worked with in the clinic and the hospital, and there were lots of things I could do. I would still be doing surgery and endoscopies. I could do women's health. My practice evolved into mostly outpatient surgery and scoping procedures. By 1999, my surgical caseload had dwindled to ninety-six cases a year.

As my case load got smaller, I didn't interact with the Sparta Hospital as often as I had before. I started working with the Tomah Hospital more, as I began providing regular surgical coverage there in 2000. I had very few concerns with the Tomah Hospital surgical services. They seemed to be willing to bend over backward to get me what I needed to provide good patient care. Tomah Memorial Hospital is an independent facility, and the medical staff is made up of physicians from both the FSH system and the Gundersen Lutheran system. The physicians work together to provide the best care for the community. It is a completely different political environment.

14
Lawsuits

I have had five malpractice lawsuits filed against me over the course of my career, and I was once sued by a nurse anesthetist for defamation of character. I have had several other patients who had less than optimal outcomes who didn't sue me.

The first malpractice case occurred my first year in Sparta. It involved a young lady with pelvic pain. She'd had pelvic pain for years and had undergone several laparoscopic procedures for fulguration (cauterizing) of sites of endometriosis. She'd had no relief. She came to me asking for a hysterectomy. She was on medical assistance, which required a second opinion by another surgeon before it would be paid for. The second opinion agreed that the procedure was indicated. The hysterectomy went well. I didn't see much evidence of endometriosis or scarring in the pelvis. Post-operatively she began to complain of pain in her flank, which was not in the area of the incision. I suspected an obstructed ureter, a known complication of hysterectomy, and did an X-ray to check for it on the second day post-op. It looked like the ureter was obstructed, and I sent the patient to La Crosse for further evaluation and treatment. They successfully drained the obstructed kidney percutaneously with a catheter through the skin, and this prevented any damage to the kidney. Later they reimplanted the ureter into the bladder, and her urinary system was able to function normally. The patient sued me for malpractice, loss of marital companionship, and disfigurement.

I think I did a good operation. Her ureters may have been pulled into abnormal positions because of scarring from her previous surgeries. I identified the known possible complication in a timely manner. I don't think I should have done anything differently. After several years of paperwork, the patient dropped the lawsuit.

The second case involved an elderly lady who presented to the Mauston Hospital with right lower quadrant pain. After examining her, I suspected acute appendicitis. I performed an appendectomy through a right-sided, up and down incision rather than the typical small oblique right lower quadrant incision because I couldn't rule out colon cancer as the cause of her pain in a woman her age, and I wanted to be able to do a definitive operation if that was what we encountered. This was before we did CT scans on all patients with abdominal pain. The surgery went well. She did have appendicitis. Apparently, post-operatively, her wound came open and was repaired by the Mauston surgeon. The patient sued me for the additional hospital costs for the wound repair. She dropped the lawsuit when we agreed to cancel my surgical charges. I think I did the right incision. It was unfortunate that her incision didn't heal. I had another patient whose wound came open several days after a gallbladder removal. I don't know why this happens. It usually only requires sewing them back together.

In 1985, I did a cholecystectomy on a twenty-eight-year-old female for chronic cholecystitis and cholelithiasis. During the surgery, I was unable to cannulate the cystic duct to do a cholangiogram. We routinely did a cholangiogram to determine if there were any stones in the common bile duct. Usually a catheter is placed in the cystic duct, which is the gallbladder duct, and dye is injected and an X-ray taken to visualize the duct system. In her case, the catheter would not go into the duct. I attempted to place a needle in the common bile duct as an alternative way to visualize the duct. No dye would go in.

I decided at that point that if the catheter and dye wouldn't go into the duct, a stone probably wouldn't either, so I didn't persist in trying to do the cholangiogram. I proceeded to remove the gallbladder. As I was dividing the thin connective tissue on the bottom side of the gallbladder, I noticed a duct-like structure coming out of the gallbladder and heading toward the bowel. Normally there is no duct in this area. As I removed the gallbladder from its bed in the liver, I noticed there were two ducts coming directly from the liver bed into the gallbladder. Usually if there are any ducts in this area, they aren't large enough to see. These were large enough to see and were draining enough bile that I thought we should tie them off so we wouldn't get a collection of bile post-op. I tied off both ducts. The rest of the procedure was routine.

That same day, driving home for lunch, it occurred to me that by taking out the gallbladder I may have disrupted the only connection this woman had between her liver and her small bowel. I suspected that she didn't have a common bile duct, had never had one, and that bile went from her liver to her small bowel through the gallbladder. Over the next two days, I watched for signs of jaundice. The liver continuously makes bile, but if the bile can't get out of the liver through the bile ducts, it backs up into the body and causes tissues to turn a yellow color—jaundice.

She did get jaundiced, and I noted in her chart that I thought she had an obstructed common bile duct. I transferred her to the Mayo Clinic for evaluation and treatment. They did a percutaneous cholangiogram by putting a catheter through the skin into a liver bile duct. Their study confirmed the biliary anatomy as I had described it. Because I had tied off the bile ducts in the liver bed, they had dilated enough to facilitate an anastomosis to the gut for drainage of the bile. She recovered well from their repair, but there is always a chance of scarring causing an obstruction at the site of anastomosis. She sued me for causing obstruction of her common bile duct.

In the 1980s, the way malpractice cases were handled in Wisconsin was with a mediation panel to try to resolve the case before going to court. The mediation panel consisted of two attorneys, two physicians, and a lay person. Each party in the suit had an attorney, and the case was presented as if in a courtroom.

My attorney and I presented the case that the patent didn't have a common bile duct so I didn't obstruct it. The Mayo Clinic would not release the cholangiogram films, preventing me from confirming the anatomy. So the case was based on my note in the chart that said she had an obstructed common bile duct post-op, and the assumption was that I caused it. The mediation panel ruled in the patient's favor, granting her thirty-five thousand dollars.

This is an example of the variable anatomy of the biliary tract. Even if I had recognized the anatomy at the time of surgery, I don't think there was anything different I could have done. The gallbladder was diseased and needed to come out. I recognized the problem, and she got appropriate treatment. Hopefully, she doesn't have any further problems.

In 1992, I did gallbladder surgery on a patient without a gallbladder. The patient presented to the emergency room with right upper quadrant pain, nausea, and vomiting. A gallbladder ultrasound was read as "findings consistent with a small contracted gallbladder." This was usually interpreted as a sign of chronic cholecystitis. She came to see me in the clinic for a pre-op exam. As part of her history, I discovered that she had had a gastric bypass. I recalled that when I was a resident it was very common for us to also remove the gallbladder from a patient who was having a gastric bypass. I asked her if the surgeons had removed her gallbladder at the time of her gastric bypass surgery. She said she didn't think so. She was a nurse, so I assumed she would know that information. I didn't check her past medical records. On the day of surgery, I initially attempted a laparoscopic approach. There were a lot of adhesions in the right upper quadrant, which was consistent with having had a gastric bypass and chronic cholecystitis. After working for some time trying to take down all the adhesions and making little progress, I decided to convert to an open procedure. Once the abdomen was open and all the adhesions were taken down, I recognized that she didn't have a gallbladder. I closed the incision, and she recovered well. In fact, after she healed up, she didn't have any more abdominal pain.

I checked her past medical records, and it was clear that her gallbladder had been removed at the time of her gastric bypass. It was also stated several times that the surgeons had shared that information with the patient. She sued me for malpractice, loss of marital companionship, and assault!

I worked with my attorney to put together the case. Once we got to the point of depositions, her attorney deposed me first. Then my attorney deposed the patient. After her deposition, her attorney wanted to settle the case. The case was settled for thirty thousand dollars.

Because there was a settlement against me, it was reported to the Wisconsin State Licensing Board. They had to decide if any disciplinary action was indicated. I had to make an appearance in Madison before the board. No action was deemed necessary. I worked with the same attorney on all of these cases, and I sought his advice on several other issues as well. We got to know each other quite well, and I learned a lot about how the legal system works.

In November of 1993, I was called to do a stat C-section. I was just arriving at the Radisson Hotel in La Crosse for a meeting on how better to meet the surgical needs of rural communities when the lady from the front desk asked, "Is there a Dr. Lottmann here? I have a phone call for her." I took the call and headed back out the door. I remember every street light was green as I traveled through La Crosse. When I got to the exit for Sparta, I called the operating room and told them where I was and to get the patient into the OR. I arrived at the hospital, went rapidly to the fourth floor, changed clothes, scrubbed briefly, and gowned up. The patient was on the OR table prepped, draped, and ready for me. The anesthetist put her to sleep, and we did the C-section and delivered the baby. I noticed the umbilical cord was limp, not firm as it usually is. The placenta floated out of the uterus. Usually I have to pull it out. The baby needed resuscitation and was transferred to La Crosse.

The mom's story was that her water broke at home, and there was a lot of blood in it. She lived only two blocks from the hospital and came to the ER right away. An obstetrical nurse did a brief assessment, and the OB provider was called. When she arrived, she examined the patient and called for a stat C-section because there was a placental abruption—the placenta had pulled free of the uterus, which means that the baby wasn't getting any oxygen.

The time from the decision to do the C-section to the start of the C-section was forty-three minutes. That was a very short time for our hospital. All our OR personnel have to come in from home. The American College of Obstetricians and Gynecologists recommends that if you are going to do obstetrics at your hospital, you should be able to start a C-section within thirty minutes of making the decision. The family sued the hospital, the OB provider, and me because we didn't do the C-section within the recommended thirty minutes, and the baby had cerebral palsy.

The case eventually ended up as a jury trial in Sparta seven years later. It was postponed several times. One postponement was because the judge was ill. Another was because my attorney was ill. The trial was scheduled for three weeks in January 2000. (There were only two other times in my career that I took three weeks off. One was to have my son in 1986 and the other was to go to Africa in 1992.)

The courtroom was full. The hospital, the OB provider, and I each had our own attorney, and the Wisconsin Patient Compensation Fund was also represented. Jury selection took a long time because the OB provider and I had been in the community a long time, and it was hard to find individuals we hadn't provided care for.

During the trial, a lot of time was spent explaining to the jury the medical facts, what they meant, and their significance to the case. I once read a book called *Jury of My Peers* by Howard C. Snider Jr., MD. It was about a jury trial malpractice case. After the trial, the defendant questioned the jurors about the case to see how much of the medically significant facts they understood. It turned out that they didn't understand very much. He makes a case for medical malpractice cases to be heard by medical people/peers of the person on trial.

One thing that really impressed me about the trial was how the judge had everyone stand when the jury entered and exited the courtroom. They were honored as the most important part of the proceedings. I think that's the way it should be.

The plaintiff's attorney brought in expert witnesses from New York and New Jersey. I got the impression that out east there are surgeons standing on street corners waiting for something to do. There aren't that many around here. I was asked, "Why didn't you get someone to cover for you if you were going to be in La Crosse?" I answered, "There was no one to ask." I was asked, "Why didn't you have one of the OB docs in La Crosse be on standby for you?" I answered, "It would take them just as long to get to Sparta." I was asked, "Why didn't you have someone standing by the helicopter?" I answered, "We couldn't tie up the helicopter for that, and truth be told, it takes the helicopter just about as long to get to Sparta."

The day I was to take the stand, I decided to wear a red suit jacket, to be bold. The Scripture I read that morning was from Ephesians 6:10–13. "Put on the whole armor of God so that you can take your stand . . . so that when the day of evil comes, you may be able to stand your ground, and after you have done everything, to stand." How appropriate! My husband also came to court that day to give me moral support.

The plaintiff's attorney asked a lot of questions. Some of them began with "supposing ..." and "assuming such and such ..." and "supposing that ..." They got so full of assumptions and suppositions that I couldn't remember what the original question was, and I said so. When all was said and done, neither the hospital, the OB provider, or I were found negligent. The jury found in our favor. (One of the obstetricians in La Crosse has done a study to find out how long it takes the OR crew at the Gundersen Lutheran Hospital to start a C-section after a decision is made. Even though all their personnel are in the hospital, it is difficult for them to begin within thirty minutes.)

The trial didn't last the full three weeks, so people asked me if I was going to spend the remaining time I had off celebrating. I told them I was going to spend it recuperating.

I learned two things from that jury trial. First, it's very hard to sit and listen to people accuse you of something and not be able to answer them right then and there. Second, doctors and lawyers think differently. I am one to take notes and so was my attorney. It surprised me at the end of the day how different our notes were after listening to the same testimony. It brought home the fact that doctors and lawyers are taught to think in completely different ways—so much so that I think we perceive things differently.

Several months later, I was asked to see a patient at a local nursing home. The nurse caring for the resident was the mother who had sued me. We managed to do what needed to be done for the resident. When we were done, we were walking down the hall together, and the only comment she made was that she had no idea I was on call so much. During the trial, my attorney had asked me to count the number of days I was on call in 1993. It was easier to count the days I wasn't on call—they were fewer—seventy-five.

A few years later, I went to a bridal shower for my nurse's daughter. Unbeknownst to me, she was marrying a relative of the family who sued me, and many members of that family were there, including the child with cerebral palsy. They sat on one side of the room, and I sat on the other. We did okay—an example of one of the "perks" of working in a small community.

Several patients come to mind who could have sued me but didn't. I was called to see a patient one evening in the ER who had abdominal pain. From his abdominal X-rays, he obviously had a large bowel obstruction with a competent ileocecal valve. Most people's ileocecal valves allow air to back up into the small bowel if there is a large bowel obstruction. His didn't, so as air was pushed by his small bowel into his large bowel, it couldn't get out. As a result, pressure built up, and if it continued, his large bowel would rupture. I took him to the OR emergently and did an exploration of his abdomen. (I remember that I had come from Jazzercise and did the operation in my tights.) The serosa or outside surface of the large bowel was already tearing. It looked like the left side of the bowel was drawn up into the left upper quadrant and was stuck there. I brought a section of the mid large bowel out to the abdominal wall as a colostomy to relieve the pressure. He recovered well.

About three months later, he came back to have the section of the bowel taken out that was causing the obstruction, and the colostomy taken down. During the anesthesia induction, he possibly aspirated some of his stomach contents into his lungs, so we immediately woke him up. We didn't do the surgery. He was transferred to La Crosse for observation. Stomach contents can do a lot of damage to the lungs. He did okay. Apparently not much got into his lungs. They proceeded to do the surgery in La Crosse. Post-operatively, he developed an abscess in the left upper quadrant. Apparently he had had one before.

His past medical history revealed that he'd had a hiatal hernia repair, at which time the spleen was injured. They took out the spleen, and post-operatively he developed a left upper quadrant abscess. This is what caused the scarring that drew the large bowel up into the left upper quadrant and caused the large bowel obstruction. He had complained of abdominal pain in the preceding several years, but no diagnosis was made as to the cause of it. I obtained copies of abdominal X-rays from several months before he had presented to the Sparta ER. They were from Illinois. I could see signs of a partial large bowel obstruction on them.

The patient and his wife consulted an attorney about possibly suing the physician who had not identified the bowel obstruction on the X-ray earlier. They were apparently advised that they didn't have much of a case there but were told they should consider suing me. They never did.

The abscess proved very hard to clear up, and he eventually ended up at the Mayo Clinic, where they had to resect the twelfth rib to open the area up for adequate drainage. The patient and his wife made frequent trips to Rochester, and while she waited for her husband to get his treatments, his wife cross-stitched a blanket for my son. We became friends. The patient and I shared the same birthday, and he came to my retirement party. I appreciate that he didn't sue me.

Soon after coming to Sparta, I was called to the ER to evaluate a girl with right lower quadrant pain. It wasn't obvious that she had appendicitis, so I proposed that we do laparoscopy to determine the cause of her pain. In females, ovarian pathology can cause pain similar to that caused by appendicitis. I placed the camera through a cannula in the belly button. I watched as I placed the trocar/cannula in the right lower quadrant. I watched as it went right into the iliac vein. In the early 1980s, the trocars didn't have safety locks. They were rigid metal rods with a pointed end. You had to try to control the depth of the puncture so you didn't damage anything.

Suddenly the field filled with blood. We rapidly pulled out the cannulas and opened the abdomen. I was able to repair the vein and stop the bleeding. I found no abnormalities in the abdomen. I put the patient on blood thinners because we had operated on a major vessel. I transferred her to La Crosse for any further treatment because I didn't normally do surgery on vessels. She did well. The patient was the granddaughter of the head nurse at the clinic. I wondered if that had anything to do with me not being sued.

I already mentioned the patient who had a common bile duct injury after I did a lap chole in 1993 when I was so hypothyroid. I had one other common bile duct injury during a lap chole. I recognized the fact that I had divided the common bile duct at the time of surgery. He apparently didn't have a cystic duct. His gallbladder sat right on his common bile duct, and I had divided that, thinking it was the cystic duct. That patient had a hard time believing that he had to have more surgery, because he felt so good post-op. He was transferred to La Crosse for repair. They apparently were unable to do the repair, so he went to Madison to the expert and was put back together. As far as I know, he has done well.

Years ago, patients stayed in the hospital quite a while after surgery. I remember a man who had bilateral hernias. We repaired both of them at the same time. He was in quite a bit of pain post-op, and it was difficult for him to move. He had a history of a blood clot in one of his legs, so it was important for him to move. On the second post-op day, he collapsed in the bathroom, and I was called emergently. We got him back to bed and connected him to monitoring equipment. His heart rate was slow. His blood pressure was low. He became unresponsive. He deteriorated before our eyes, and there didn't seem to be anything we could do about it. He had gone into third-degree heart block, and we tried to treat it with external pacing without success. I took him to X-ray and tried to place an internal pacing wire. Still we got no response. I believe he had developed a blood clot in his leg that had broken loose and traveled to his lungs, where it had acted like a plug obstructing blood flow. The only way to treat that is to open the chest and remove the blood clot. We were not equipped to do that. He died. The family never wanted to see me for anything after that, but they didn't sue.

The only other patient that I operated on who died unexpectedly post-op was a patient I did a hemorrhoidectomy on. Even simple operations can be stressful. I think he had a heart attack.

I have had inadvertent bladder injuries in two patients. One was a hysterectomy patient. I recognized it and called the urologist to confirm that what I was going to do to repair it was right. He asked me if there was any damage to the ureters. I then identified that there was, but we didn't have any stents to use to do a repair. The urologist came from La Crosse with the stents while the patient was still on the operating table, and I helped him with the repair. Unfortunately, the Foley catheter came out on post-op day two and wasn't replaced right away. The patient developed a vaginal fistula, which means a hole developed between her bladder and vagina, and she leaked urine from her vagina. After several weeks of healing, she was taken back to the OR by the urologist to repair the fistula. Apparently her surgery was very challenging. She ended up with a small bladder, but the urine went to the right place. The second bladder injury occurred during a C-section. The ob-gyn doc helped me repair that one.

One patient threatened to sue me unless I paid him some money. He had presented with right lower quadrant pain that I didn't think was appendicitis. I sent him to La Crosse so they could help decide what was wrong. They apparently did a CT scan, decided it was appendicitis, and took his appendix out. He sent me a letter that said if I paid him fifteen thousand dollars, he wouldn't sue me for not making the diagnosis. I didn't respond, and I didn't hear from him again.

The defamation of character lawsuit happened in 1998. The hospital needed to hire a nurse anesthetist. The candidate they hired apparently came with her own contract, which listed three reasons why she could be fired. Within a very short period of time, everyone in the OR sensed there was something amiss. I couldn't put my finger on just what it was, but the atmosphere in the OR became very tense. I observed the anesthetist having difficulty doing spinals, although she said she could do them well. She said things that I thought were inappropriate in front of patients. We would discuss the type of anesthesia we were going to use on a particular patient the night before the case, and the next morning it was as if we hadn't talked about it at all. I didn't know exactly what was wrong, but I knew it was putting patients at risk.

I spoke with the hospital administrator about my concerns, and she suggested we sit down together and talk. So the administrator, the anesthetist, and I sat down to try to figure things out. The anesthetist and I agreed to try some things differently—but nothing changed. It got to the point where I didn't trust her. I didn't trust what was going on at the head of the OR table behind the drape during surgery. I didn't know if during a procedure she would do what I wanted done for the patient. It was as if she didn't hear what I was saying. In a small hospital where there is one surgeon and one anesthetist, their relationship and communication are critical.

After what I thought was an adequate trial I informed the hospital administrator that it wasn't working; I wasn't willing to do surgery with her anymore. The best I could do in explaining the situation was that our philosophies of how to care for patients in the OR were so different we couldn't work together. To emphasize my decision, I personally transported an appendicitis patient to La Crosse for his surgery rather than do it in Sparta in an unsafe environment.

The administrator apparently told the anesthetist that since I wasn't willing to work with her, they would have to let her go. This situation was not one of the three reasons she had listed in her contract as just cause for termination, so the anesthetist sued the hospital for breach of contract, and she sued me for defamation of character for fifteen million dollars.

The anesthetist had apparently applied for a job at another small hospital in the area and was not hired. I think she thought I had told them something about her. The only person I had talked to about her was the surgeon in Tomah. I saw him at a surgery conference in Minneapolis, and he asked me, "How is the new anesthetist working out?" I told him, "It isn't." That's all I said.

I assume she didn't get the job because the OR supervisor in Sparta, Sister Mary Aquin, was a member of the board of directors at the other hospital where she applied. Both hospitals were owned by the Sisters of Perpetual Adoration. The lawsuit progressed through her having three different attorneys. I was deposed three times.

Defamation of character is a civil charge. It is not a malpractice issue, so my malpractice insurance wouldn't cover any claim she won. I would have to pay that out of my own pocket. However, the situation was considered a peer review issue, so my malpractice insurance did cover the attorney fees.

When we finally got to the point of her deposition, where my attorney and the hospital attorney asked her questions, the problem clarified itself. The anesthetist's response to any question was completely unrelated to the question. I remember all of us sitting around the conference table, and when she answered a question, we would all look at each other with furrowed brows as if to say, "Where did that come from?"

The anesthetist eventually dropped the lawsuit against me, but she did have a case of breach of contract against the hospital. They had signed her contract that stated the three reasons she could be fired. I don't know how much money exchanged hands there. I did get a thank-you note from the hospital administrator applauding me for standing my ground and preventing any patient injury.

Later, out of curiosity, I called the administrator of the hospital where the anesthetist had worked before coming to Sparta. He described the exact same scenario happening there. I suspect this was the way this anesthetist made a living. Didn't the Sparta hospital administrator check references before hiring this anesthetist? I don't know. I bet it was done for all hires after that.

15

Interesting Cases—Obstetrics

I have delivered over five hundred babies by C-section. Some of those procedures were very memorable.

In 1985, before it was routine to do prenatal ultrasounds, I did a C-section on a patient of one of the older OB providers. After delivering the baby, the family practice doc took the baby to the warmer to examine and care for it while I closed the incision. I had delivered the placenta, but the uterus didn't seem to be clamping down as it should. I expressed my concern, and the family doc said, "Maybe there's another one in there." And sure enough, there was! We had twins! After I delivered the second baby and placenta, the uterus clamped down nicely, and I could finish the procedure. That kind of thing doesn't happen anymore because with ultrasounds, everyone knows if there is "more than one in there."

Recently my husband and I attended a high school graduation party for a girl I had delivered by C-section. While there, the girl's mother pointed out to me that I had delivered all five of her children by C-section. Today it's not often that a woman has five C-sections, and how often is it that the same surgeon did all five?

C-sections are divided into three categories based on the urgency of the situation. In the first, the surgeon is called for an emergency

C-section because the baby or the mother or both are in distress. It can be when the mother is bleeding or has the disease of pregnancy (eclampsia) or when the placenta has pulled loose. Or it can be when the baby's umbilical cord is over the top of the baby's head so that with every contraction it is pinched against the mother's pelvis and the blood supply to the baby is cut off. Or it can be when the baby's umbilical cord is around the baby's neck and acts like a tether so the baby can't come down and the blood supply can't flow to the baby. We do a C-section as soon as possible to save the baby's and/or the mother's life. It's called a stat C-section.

I remember one such call early in my time in Sparta. I was providing C-section coverage for a hospital an hour away. When I got the call, I jumped in our Corvette and drove one hundred miles per hour down the freeway. Minutes count! I ran to the OR and, without changing clothes, put on the gown and gloves. They had the patient ready, and as soon as I got the scalpel in my hand, they put her to sleep and we did the procedure. Mom and baby did okay. Rarely is it necessary to skip my changing clothes or scrubbing. I think it only happened one other time.

In the second situation, a C-section is called because labor isn't progressing as it should. This can be because of an abnormality of the mother or the baby. The situation isn't considered as critical, but it is urgent. We do this type of C-section when it is called, day or night.

The third type is a scheduled C-section. These occur most commonly when the mother has had a C-section before or when it's her first baby and it's a breech presentation (the butt is coming first).

We used to allow women to go into labor if they had a previous C-section for a breech presentation. If the uterine incision is horizontal it is considered supported by the pelvis and will hold together even with subsequent labor. That isn't always true. I was called to do a stat C-section on a woman who had severe abdominal pain following a contraction. She had had a previous C-section. When I opened the abdomen, I saw the baby's face behind a thin membrane. The uterus had ruptured, and I was looking at the amniotic sac. Luckily she wasn't bleeding much. We cut open the sac and delivered the baby without a problem. We then closed the uterus. Any future deliveries for her would be done by C-section.

I remember doing an urgent C-section early on in my career for a failure to progress. There had been no prenatal ultrasound. Upon delivering the baby, it was obvious why labor had not progressed. The baby was an anencephalic. It had no crown to the head. Sister Mary Aquin took the baby to another room and baptized it and attended it for its brief life.

I have done two C-sections where the baby was dead on delivery. Those are really hard. What is supposed to be a very happy event is tragic. The lack of the sound of the baby's cry is ominous.

One day I was called to do an emergency C-section in the middle of afternoon clinic. It was for a prolapsed cord—the umbilical cord was over the baby's head. The OB provider was the only other doctor in the clinic that day, so they had to close the clinic; we both had to go to the OR.

It takes a little time to set up the OR, and during that time, to prevent the uterine contractions from closing off all the blood supply to the baby with a prolapsed cord, someone has to push the baby's head back up. So, picture this: as the patient is being moved to the OR, there is someone else on the cart between the patient's legs pushing on the baby's head. That person keeps a hand in there as we move the mother to the OR bed, prep and drape, and get ready. The person pushing on the baby's head is under the drapes and keeps pushing until I deliver the baby. From my perspective, it seems funny to feel fingers when I reach into the pelvis to deliver the baby's head. I actually met one of the nurse midwives in this kind of situation. She was hoping I wasn't going to cut her fingers.

Traditionally the incision made in the uterus was vertical. That incision will not tolerate future labor so is always a repeat C-section. Today uterine incisions are usually done horizontally low down on the uterus so other pelvic structures can support the area and the uterus can tolerate future labor. Only if the baby is in a transverse lie—is lying crossways in the uterus instead of head or butt down—is a vertical incision on the uterus indicated. It's amazing how tight the baby can be in that uterus. Once I encountered a baby in a transverse lie when I had a horizontal incision. I could not get that baby to come down so I could deliver it no matter what I tried. I had to extend my incision vertically to get the baby out. Lesson learned.

I have had very few baby injuries during C-sections. They usually occur because you are cutting with a knife very near the baby. I've had a few small skin cuts. They heal up amazingly fast in newborns. The worst injury was a broken arm. I was helping another surgeon learn how to do C-sections. I was standing on the opposite side of the table from where I usually stand. Once the incision was made into the uterus, there was a lot of bleeding. The only way to stop bleeding in this situation is to get the baby and placenta out and allow the uterus to clamp down. I didn't think the other surgeon was moving fast enough, so I reached in to deliver the baby. Being on the wrong side of the table for me, I put undo pressure on the baby's upper arm. I felt and heard the bone break. My stomach went to my knees. The rest of the procedure went fine. I reported the broken arm to the mother and the family practice doc. They taped the baby's arm to her side and within a week she was moving it normally. Babies do heal rapidly.

I have done a lot of C-sections for the Amish. They usually use a lay midwife for their deliveries and don't come to the hospital unless they are having a problem. They come because they have been in labor a long time or are bleeding. We have not seen them prenatally, so we usually don't know what we are getting into. They could be a challenge, but they always recovered rapidly.

I would frequently forget to see my C-section patients post-op because they weren't sick. They were healthy and usually did very well. We had standard post-op orders, and the nurses did a good job caring for the patients. They would call me if they had any questions and to remind me to come see the patient.

I remember one Christmas Eve I was called to Hillsboro to do a C-section. I usually don't play music in the OR, but this being Christmas, I decided to bring some Christian tapes along. Once I got there, I learned that the patient was Jewish and her name was Mary. We didn't play my music, and we delivered her first child, a baby boy.

I also remember a patient who needed a C-section who had two beautiful dragons tattooed on her abdomen. They were mirror images of one another, and she didn't want me to cut across them. So we did a vertical midline incision and left them intact.

I did one stat C-section when I had a newly-broken foot. I had slipped on the floor when entering the clinic that morning because my shoes were wet. I twisted my right foot under me and felt a twinge but didn't think much of it. I didn't fall down. As the morning wore on, my foot swelled up and began to hurt. I eventually saw one of my colleagues, who suggested we get an X-ray. It showed that I had fractured the base of my fifth metatarsal. It was not displaced, but now it was too swollen to put a cast on. They recommended that I stay off of it the rest of the day, and in the morning we would put on a cast. I remember giving a potential new doc a tour of the hospital that day while sitting in a wheelchair being pushed around by the elderly Sister Mary Aquin. I went home and put my foot up. In the early evening, I got called for a stat C-section. I could maneuver by walking on my heel, so I got to the OR okay. The challenge came when I had scrubbed my hands and had to get into the OR without touching anything. Staff provided me with a stool on wheels to scoot into the OR. During the case I rested my foot on the base of the OR table. The surgery went well. Then I went home and put my foot up again. Doctors put on the cast the next morning, and work went on.

Toward the end of my career, I was doing C-sections on women I had delivered by C-section.

One Friday in 2000, when I was covering Sparta and Tomah, I did four C-sections in one day. One was scheduled, but the other three were emergent or urgent. I told the fourth patient that I was well practiced for the procedure.

One C-section was memorable because of what the OB provider said. Once the baby is delivered, the OB provider takes him or her to the warmer for a cleanup and checkup. After a while on this particular occasion, I asked how things were going, and the OB provider said, "Frankly, I don't give a damn!" I was surprised. Usually this provider is all business and proper. What could he mean by what he said? Then I realized that it was a baby boy whom the parents had decided to name Rhett—like the character in *Gone with the Wind*. Then it made sense.

Part of obstetrics is dealing with miscarriages; the baby dies in the uterus. In the great majority of cases, the miscarriage occurs in early pregnancy, and the mother's body gets rid of the tissue on its own. Sometimes, however, the dead tissue doesn't pass, and a D&C is required. We dilate the cervix just enough to get an instrument into the uterus and then scrape the lining of the uterus with the curved blade on the end of the instrument, dull first and, if necessary, then a sharp one. I have done many D&Cs. My worst fear was that the diagnosis would not be right and that I would actually be terminating a viable pregnancy with my procedure. I was always relieved when I saw black tissue coming out. That meant that the baby was dead. Sometimes I could identify body parts. I didn't like these procedures, but they needed to be done.

Later in pregnancy, if the baby is bigger and dies, it is usually delivered by giving the patient drugs to induce labor. It is a very difficult time for the mother because she has to go through labor knowing that the baby is dead.

I was presented with a patient whose baby had died, and the entire baby had not been delivered. Apparently the patient presented to the clinic for a regularly scheduled prenatal visit. On examination she was found to have the baby's legs hanging out of the cervix. The OB provider determined that the baby was not alive and apparently tried to deliver the baby by pulling on the legs. She was successful in delivering the body but the head tore off and remained in the uterus.

That's when I was called in. They wanted me to deliver the head. The baby's head is the largest part of its body, so even though the body had come out of the cervix, the cervix wasn't dilated enough to get the head out. Under general anesthesia, I used the largest clamps we could find to further dilate the cervix. It was not easy. It seemed like I was doing a medieval procedure, pulling and stretching with gross instruments. As I was doing this, the OB provider stuck her head in the door of the OR and said, "Could you deliver the head intact so I can sew it back on the body so the mom can see the baby?" How was I supposed to do that?

At that time, my son was into Teenage Mutant Ninja Turtles, and as I palpated the head in the uterus, it felt like one of his ninja turtle balls. I could feel the face. Eventually I got a good hold on the head and closed the clamp tight. This crushed the head, but I was able to pull it out. I don't know if the OB provider tried to sew it back on the body, but I got it out. Thankfully, the patient didn't bleed at all during this ordeal.

I would also be called to do a D&C if a patient continued to bleed following delivery. That usually occurs because some of the placenta doesn't come out. It is dangerous to do a D&C right after delivery because the uterine wall is so thin that it's easy to poke an instrument through it. I usually tried to get my hand in there and use my fingers to scrape the uterus. Fingers are more blunt than the instruments. I remember one case where the patient bled so much that she used up most of her clotting factors and went into DIC (disseminated intravascular coagulation). When you use up your clotting factors, you bleed more. We recognized the situation and sent her to La Crosse for care. She did well. She sent me and the OB provider beautiful floral arrangements as a thank you.

I was presented with one case of an inverted uterus. Basically, the uterus is inside out and sticking out of the vagina. I knew in cows the vet usually just pushed it back in. What do you do in women? I got out a book, and it said you make a fist and push it back in. So that is what I did. It worked! I packed the vagina to keep it in.

The Sparta Hospital no longer provides OB services. At my retirement party, a longtime employee of the hospital shared that I was one of the reasons the hospital was able to provide OB services for as long as it did.

One procedure we did not do at the Sparta Hospital, a Catholic institution, was tubal ligations. They can be done postpartum—within twenty-four hours of delivery—or electively, at least six weeks postdelivery. I did tubals at the Tomah Hospital. I did postpartum tubals through a small incision just below the belly button because that is where the dome of the uterus is right after delivery. I did elective tubals through a small incision just above the pubic bone because that is where the dome of the uterus usually is. I would make an incision just big enough to allow my finger and a long clamp inside the abdomen. I would find the dome of the uterus and slide my finger to one side and hook the tube. I would then grasp it with the clamp and bring it out of my incision. I would follow it to its end to confirm it was the tube and then I would take a section of the middle of the tube out and tie the two cut ends shut. I would do the same thing on the other side. I reasoned that this was the most definitive procedure, and it caused the least amount of damage to the tube. If the patient in the future changed her mind and wanted her tubes put back together again, there was good tissue to work with. I never did laparoscopic tubals because my incision was so small and the procedure was so fast. It usually took me about ten minutes to do.

When they first started doing laparoscopic tubals, one of the techniques was to lift the midsection of the tube and put a band around it. I had a patient who presented with pelvic pain. We determined that there was a mass near her ovary and did surgery to take it out. On exploration, I found the loop of tube above the band greatly dilated. This was the mass. Apparently, the tube had continued to secrete its normal fluids, but there was no place for them to go, so they collected in the tube, causing it to dilate and cause pain. Removing her tube relieved her pain. This case reinforced for me a basic principle of surgery. Any mucosa-lined tubular organ (think bowel) has to have a place for secretions to drain or they accumulate and cause other problems.

I have to admit I did a few tubals at the Sparta Hospital. If we ended up doing a C-section on a patient who wanted a tubal, I would do it when I had the abdomen open. I would send Sister Mary Aquin out of the room on an errand and quickly do the deed. She wouldn't find out about it until she saw the operative report. I always dictated that it had been done. There wasn't much she could do about it then. Eventually, the hospital allowed tubals.

You may have heard of flesh-eating bacterial infections; they sometimes make the news. Thankfully they are rare. The one case I saw during my career was in a patient who had had a laparoscopic tubal done by another surgeon. Just two days after her procedure, she presented to the ER with gray fluid leaking from the incision at the belly button. The surrounding tissue was slightly pink, pale, and very tender. I suspected necrotizing fasciitis and sent her to La Crosse for debridement. She did well. We don't understand why these infections develop, but they can be devastating.

16

Trauma

Early in my career, I took care of a lot of trauma patients. I was very comfortable doing that because of my training at St. Paul Ramsey. I liked trauma. I was called to the ER in Sparta for all major traumas. This was before ER docs were required to take ATLS. Typically, I would intubate the patient if needed, put in the IV if it was a difficult one, put in the chest tube if needed, put in the Foley catheter, and do a peritoneal lavage if indicated. I worked my way around the patient. As more ER docs became certified in ATLS, I was called less often.

I operated on several gunshot victims. One patient was a hunter whose gun went off while he was going through a fence. He shot off the front of his right thigh. I did a debridement and skin graft. He did well. He was my cleaning lady's husband. After that, I was acutely aware of whether I was on call on opening day of deer-hunting season.

We saw many car accident victims. If they had a head injury or orthopedic injuries, they would go to La Crosse. But if their injury was in the abdomen, we could care for them. We initially did splenectomys and splenorrhaphys (spleen repairs) and repaired liver lacerations. Once the standard of practice became observation for these types of injuries, they all went to La Crosse for care. They had the blood products that would be needed if they continued to bleed. They also had better CT scanners to follow the patients.

One patient I will never forget had evidence of a head injury and acted like a head injury patient following a car accident. She was agitated, restless, trying to sit up, fighting us, noncooperative, out of it. Her vital signs were normal. Her young daughter's only injury was a forehead laceration. We started an IV and ran it slowly to prevent brain swelling and transferred her to La Crosse. I did not do a peritoneal lavage. The patient apparently died on the way to La Crosse from a ruptured spleen. Apparently the agitation was from hypoxia. How could I have missed that?

There were two auto accidents at the street corner less than a block from my home. One was a car full of elderly women who pulled out in front of a semi. The accident killed all but one of the women. She was in severe straits, so we took her to the OR immediately. I intubated her because anesthesia wasn't there yet. I had a nurse bag her while we opened her abdomen. The spleen was ruptured, and even though we were able to stop the bleeding, we couldn't save her.

The other accident was another car that pulled out in front of a semi. This time the semi swerved to avoid the car and tipped over. It was a load of sheet metal, and it sounded like a building fell down. The cab of the semi was essentially upside down in the ditch. I went out in my pajamas to see if I could help. The driver crawled out of the cab, and I rode in the ambulance with him to the hospital, which was less than five minutes away. He had minimal injuries. So there I was in the ER in my pajamas with nothing to do. Someone eventually gave me a ride home.

Another car accident victim was a patient who was going home after having had brain surgery at the Mayo Clinic. His wife said the last thing the doctor told him when he left was not to get into a car accident or bump his head. Well, there was an accident. The patient didn't have many injuries, but he apparently had bumped his head and the scalp incision had opened up. He must have had his head on the ground because there was grass stuck in the wire sutures that were holding his skull in place. I called the neurosurgeon at the Mayo Clinic, and he told me to give the patient antibiotics and clean him up and close the incision and send him back. We used a lot of irrigation and picked all the grass out of the sutures. I sewed the scalp back together without anesthesia because it was still numb from the surgery. Then he went back to Rochester. I never did hear how he did.

A large elderly lady was the driver of a small car that was struck on the passenger side. She was severely injured and had crepitus (air in the subcutaneous tissue) on her right side, suggesting a lung injury. After intubating her, I attempted to put in a chest tube on the right. After cutting through the skin and subcutaneous tissue I couldn't find the fifth rib. In fact I couldn't find any rib or chest wall. All I could feel was the lung. I found her entire chest wall on the underside of her arm. We were not able to resuscitate her.

My best save, I believe, was an eighteen-year-old girl from Massachusetts. She, along with four friends, was traveling across the country to go to school in the Northwest. They were in an accident on the freeway. She was the driver. The others were all killed. She had a fracture of her left upper arm but no other injuries. She was awake and alert, and her only complaint was it felt like she had peanut butter in the back of her throat. I did a chest X-ray and convinced myself that her mediastinum, the central portion of her chest above her heart, was widened. That was a sign of a ruptured aorta. The severity of the accident also suggested a rapid deceleration. I transferred her to La Crosse, and they did an angiogram. She did have a ruptured aorta, and they repaired it. The feeling of peanut butter in the back of her throat I think was swelling from the blood in the mediastinum tracking upward. Apparently her father was a cardiologist, and he sent me a letter thanking me for making that diagnosis.

There is a meat-packing plant south of Sparta, and we would sometimes see injured patients from there. One gentleman presented with abdominal pain after being pinned against a loading dock by a truck. The corner of the loading dock had been pushed into his abdomen. His peritoneal lavage was positive, so I took him to the OR. There were about two units of blood in the abdomen but no active bleeding. I identified a bruised right iliac artery. I didn't pick it up because I didn't have any material to repair an artery. We took him to the recovery room, where he lost his right femoral pulse, suggesting a further problem with that iliac artery. We sent him to La Crosse, where they found another two units of blood in his abdomen and repaired the artery.

Another patient from the plant presented with a chest injury. Apparently a bull wouldn't come out of the truck, so he went in to get him. The bull got the man in a corner and pummeled him repeatedly until someone shot the bull. The patient was conscious when he arrived in the ER but complained of chest pain. His entire chest was unstable. I put chest tubes in each side but couldn't find a solid rib to push against to do it. I had to cut all the way in to place the tube. He did well, but I think it hurt him to breathe for a long time.

Other injuries we would frequently see were farm injuries. One patient presented with a power take-off injury of his right leg. His pant leg had caught in the power take-off and essentially twisted all the soft tissues of his lower leg around the bone by 180 degrees. There was a small laceration on the front of his lower leg, and muscle was bulging out because of all the pressure in the leg. He had a compartment syndrome, and it needed to be relieved *immediately*. He had just been to Burger King where he had eaten two burgers and a shake, so his stomach was full—we couldn't put him to sleep. We did a spinal anesthetic, and he had no more pain. Following a picture in the book, I did a four-compartment fasciotomy to relieve the pressure and then went with him in the ambulance to La Crosse. His vein had to be repaired, but the artery was intact. The nerve was stretched but didn't need repair. He recovered with only a little foot drop from the nerve damage.

I have sewn up many chain saw injuries. They are like putting a puzzle back together, trying to find where all the pieces fit. People tend to take the guards off the machines. The saw catches on something or bounces off the wood and can cut almost anywhere.

As time went on, I was called less and less for trauma patients. The ER physicians were trained in ATLS, liver and spleen injuries were observed instead of being operated on, and patients could be transported by helicopter. Sometimes the helicopter picked them up at the scene of the accident and took them to the trauma hospital in La Crosse so we never even saw the patient in the Sparta ER. As I got older, I didn't really miss being called for the trauma cases. I still liked to hear about them, though.

17
Interesting Cases—General Surgery

Early in my career, I did stomach surgery. The more people began to use gastric acid inhibitors, the less stomach surgery was needed. A patient with severe arthritis had recurrent gastric outlet obstruction because of scarring from ulcers. I did an antrectomy (removed the distal stomach) and vagotomy (cut the vagus nerves). She did well. Another patient had a gastric lymphoma. I did a large gastric resection (removed most of her stomach), and she recovered well despite being elderly.

The hospital administrator asked me one time if I did highly selective vagotomies. I had never done one in residency because they started doing them after my training. I never found a need to do one. One patient had previously had a Whipple operation for pancreatic cancer. He had survived more than twelve years since his surgery. I don't think he had adenomatous cancer, because he survived so long. But he developed an anastomotic ulcer that wouldn't heal. So I redid the gastric anastomotic part (where they sewed the bowel to his stomach) of his Whipple. He did really well.

As the number of gastric surgeries dwindled, the number of gastric endoscopies increased. I recall one upper endoscopy I did for a patient who had swallowed a diamond ring. He apparently was attempting to steal it, but it got stuck in his esophagus and started to cause pain, so he told someone about it. He was brought in by the police. The ring needed to be removed. I didn't have any endoscopic instruments big enough to grab a ring, so I decided to put the cleaning brush into the scope and bend the end up as a hook. I pulled it tight up against the end of the scope so it wouldn't cause any damage on the way in. We sedated the patient—or I should say we tried to sedate the patient. After giving him the maximum dose of the usual meds, he was still wide awake. He agreed to proceed, so I numbed up the back of his throat and put the scope in. I pushed the ring into his stomach and successfully caught the ring on the hook of the cleaning brush. Then I simply removed the scope. The ring was retrieved, and I gave it to the policeman who was standing at my elbow. In the recovery area, the patient had a good nap.

Soon after we began doing upper endoscopy, I learned of a method to do a gastrostomy (a small hole into the stomach through the abdominal wall to use for drainage or for feeding) using the scope. It involved passing the scope through the mouth and into the stomach, numbing the skin and making a small incision in the abdominal wall over the stomach where we could see the light from the scope, putting an IV catheter into the stomach through the incision, passing a string through the catheter into the stomach, grasping the string with the biopsy forceps, and pulling the string out of the mouth by withdrawing the scope. The string was then tied to the gastrostomy tube, and by pulling on the string at the abdominal wall, the tube was pulled through the mouth, through the esophagus, through the stomach, and out the incision in the abdominal wall. The tube had a cap on the end so it sat snuggly up against the inside stomach wall. A stitch was placed and tied around the tube on the outside to keep the stomach tight against the inside of the abdominal wall. A baby-bottle nipple was placed over the tube to help it sit at a ninety-degree angle from the abdominal wall. The gastrostomy could be used right away. Initially, we used a number one silk thread, a tapered IV needle of an older vintage, a capped tube, and the baby-bottle nipple. Now all the supplies you need to do an endoscopic gastrostomy come in a kit.

I didn't do much vascular surgery. I preferred to let the surgeons in La Crosse do it. But two patients taught me a lot about vascular disease. The first patient was a lady who had had both legs amputated just below the groin, and her wounds didn't want to heal. She would come to clinic frequently for debridement. She had bad heart disease too.

The second patient also already had bilateral leg amputations and presented with an acute thrombotic occlusion of an axillary artery (a blood clot in the artery to his arm). If the blood clot wasn't removed, he could lose his arm. I removed the blood clot without much difficulty, and he was forever grateful.

I taught myself how to use a Doppler ultrasound to evaluate patients for arterial or venous disease. It is amazing what your vessels sound like.

Most of my vascular surgery involved doing amputations of necrotic toes and legs. There is not much to do to amputate a toe. You just want to make sure that if you remove it at the joint, you rough up the surface of the remaining bone so it doesn't continue to produce synovial fluid.

To remove a leg, you have to pay attention to how much soft tissue you have left so you can close the wound over the cut bone with sufficient soft tissue to cushion it. I usually cut the bone with a "gigli" saw. It's a braided wire with loops on the end that you connect to handles. You pull side to side with your arms wide. It works very well and cuts very fast. No fancy equipment needed. I remember one instance where we did an above-the-knee amputation on the weekend, and the lab didn't have refrigerator or freezer space for such a large specimen. They put it in a bag and put it outside on the second-story window ledge. It was winter, so it kept well until it was sent to pathology on Monday.

I did one arm amputation. It wasn't because of vascular disease. The patient was a nursing-home resident who had had a stroke. She could not use her right arm and had developed a contracture at the elbow, so her fist was right up against her cheek. She then developed a repetitive jerky movement that caused her to continually hit herself in her face. No matter what they did to restrain the arm, they couldn't stop it. We did an above-the-elbow amputation, and she was much more comfortable.

Appendectomies

I did many appendectomies. I never did them laparoscopically because the incision I used was so small I couldn't justify the additional cost of using the laparoscopic equipment. Early on, I did an appendectomy for appendicitis, and an adenocarcinoma of the appendix was incidentally found on pathology. It apparently caused the obstruction that caused the appendicitis. We did a right hemicolectomy, and the patient has done fine. I did an appendectomy on a colleague of mine and found a normal appendix. Nearby was a wedge of omentum that had died, and that was what was causing the pain. I also did an appendectomy on a famous country singer's bus driver. The country singer was performing at the County Fair at the time.

One patient presented with what looked like a hernia at the site of his previous appendectomy. That would be very unusual, because the appy incision doesn't cut muscle. There are three layers of muscle in the abdominal wall where we do the appy incision. The muscle fibers of each layer run in a different direction from those of the other layers. To get inside the abdomen, we go between the muscle fibers of all three layers. When we close the wound, the muscle fibers fall back together and reinforce each other. Upon exploration of this patient's wound, he was found to have a sterile abscess, but no hernia. All the sutures that had been placed in the external muscle layer and were supposed to dissolve were still there and were causing a chronic irritation. Once they were removed, they actually floated out, the wound healed nicely.

I did one appendectomy in Hillsboro. I went to Hillsboro one day a week for elective surgical cases and to see patients in clinic. It just so happened that this patient presented to the ER with appendicitis the day I was scheduled, so they asked me to see him. We took out his appendix as the last procedure of my day, and I went home. Immediately post-operatively he complained of a lot of pain. The nurses gave him morphine, but it didn't seem to be helping. His blood pressure was low, but they attributed that to the morphine. Eventually the recovery room nurse decided that something serious was going on and called me. I live an hour away. I found out that another surgeon was in a community closer to Hillsboro so I asked him to go see the patient and do what needed to be done until I got there. When I arrived, they had the patient back in the OR, prepped, draped, and ready for surgery. We opened his abdomen, and there was some free blood, but what was most impressive was a large retroperitoneal (behind the bowel) hematoma. It was about the size of a football. Usually you can't find a bleeder in a hematoma. But I knew where I had been operating earlier. So after removing as much clot as I could, I put my finger at the base of the appendiceal stump and rolled the small bowel over onto my hand to look behind it, and there was the bleeder. The hematoma had torn the small bowel mesentery off the retroperitoneum, so I could lift the small bowel like that. We tied off the bleeder and closed the patient up. Who would have thought that the small appendiceal artery could bleed enough to cause pressure to tear tissues like that? The patient recovered without further incident.

One patient presented with all the signs and symptoms of appendicitis, but on exploration the appendix was normal. When you do an appy incision, the scar leads the next surgeon to believe that the appendix is gone, so even if the appendix is normal, we take it out. When you find a normal appendix, you usually look around to see if something else is wrong. This patient's small bowel wasn't normal. It was all inflamed. He had inflammatory bowel disease. After taking out his appendix, I wondered if the bowel would heal if I simply closed the hole. I didn't want things to leak into the abdominal cavity, so I put a Foley catheter in the appendiceal stump and blew up the balloon. I pulled the catheter out as a drain and closed the skin. He went to La Crosse for definitive surgery for his inflammatory bowel disease.

Hernias

There are many ways to repair inguinal hernias. Surgeons usually do the one they are most familiar with and the one that has worked well for them. I did McVay repairs. (I didn't use mesh unless the patient didn't have enough good tissue to do the repair.) I had very good results with this repair and very few recurrences. It did require the patient not to do any lifting over twenty pounds for four weeks after surgery.

One patient had inguinal hernia repairs done on both sides but at different times. One side was done with a mesh plug, and I did the other side without mesh. He chronically complained of discomfort on the side with the mesh but never had any problem with the side I repaired.

I did a bilateral inguinal hernia repair on an elderly gentleman. He did well initially but then developed infection on one side. It was the side I had done first. The same repair was done on both sides. On the infected side the row of sutures floated out one day as we were doing the dressing change. The second side did fine. You would think that if the first side got infected, the second side would too, because we used all the same instruments. Perhaps there was something else that made the first side susceptible to infection. Maybe it was a reaction to the suture material. But again, I used the same kind of suture on both sides. It still puzzles me.

One hernia patient presented to the clinic with his family. They had been trying to get him to get his hernia repaired for a long time. It was now becoming more symptomatic. It wasn't until he learned who I was married to that he agreed to the surgery. He apparently knew my husband and his parents, and that convinced him he could trust me.

One hernia repair was memorable not because of who the patient was or what procedure I was doing; it was because of my condition. I had been having some abnormal uterine bleeding. I was wearing a large pad, but during the procedure I started bleeding rather heavily. By the time I finished the hernia repair (it usually took me about an hour), I had soaked through the pad, my underwear, and my inner pant legs. Blood was dripping into my shoes. I bled way more than the patient did. I couldn't quit because there was no one else to finish the procedure. When I was done, I laid down and put my feet up and the bleeding slowed. It was a good thing we had an all-female OR crew. They could relate.

Recurrent hernias can be a challenge because you have to go through scar tissue, and it's difficult to identify important structures. Usually you can simply find the hole and close it. The risk is damage to the vas deferens or the blood supply to the testes in men. Once I had a patient who had had two previous hernia repairs. I anticipated there would be a lot of scar tissue in the area. I was aware of an alternative approach—a Nyhus repair—that would allow me to approach the area of the hernia from above through normal tissue. I thought that would be best for this patient, but I had never done one before. I read up on the procedure and did it with the book open in the OR. It went well.

I did most of my hernia repairs under local anesthesia with IV sedation. Patients tolerated this very well. I used an anesthetic solution that was half-short-acting local and half-long-acting local anesthetic. If I was careful to infiltrate all layers with anesthetic, they were comfortable for a good twelve hours. I advised them to start taking pain medication when they first began to feel any discomfort, and they were able to adequately control their pain.

I repaired a couple of incarcerated femoral hernias—one in a man and one in a woman. They are much less common than inguinal hernias. I also identified and repaired one Spigelian hernia. You'll have to look that one up.

I never did laparoscopic hernia repairs. After they became more common, if I had a patient with bilateral inguinal hernias or a recurrent hernia or a hernia in a patient, such as a farmer, who couldn't be off of work for very long, I referred him to La Crosse for a laparoscopic repair. I thought they would get a better procedure from someone who did them often.

Similarly, I would repair small ventral or umbilical hernias but would refer large ones to La Crosse for laparoscopic repair.

Gallbladder Removals

I was trained to do open cholecystectomies (removal of the gallbladder). In the late 1980s, surgeons started to do them laparoscopically. In 1990, I went to a course sponsored by a school, Rush Presbyterian St. Luke's, rather than an equipment company to learn how to do them. There was an instructor for every three students. We did procedures on pigs. I found I had no trouble adapting to the new approach. There was one surgeon in the group who couldn't seem to master the eye/hand coordination. He was in the middle of his career and wasn't able to do the new procedure. That was sad.

After my training we did trial runs in the OR so everyone would know how to do the procedure. The hospital didn't own the laparoscopic equipment, but there was a company that would rent out the equipment for a day. An equipment representative would come and set up the equipment. He was a great resource when I found myself in difficult situations. He had seen a lot more of these procedures than I had.

We decided to try to schedule two procedures a day to make the equipment rental more cost effective. We were ready. We did two procedures the first day. They went well. We were planning on putting an article in the local paper about how we were offering this new procedure at the hospital. Unfortunately, one of the patients developed a stroke the evening following the surgery, so we didn't think it appropriate to publish the article.

We went on to do many lap choles. They were actually fun to do, like playing video games. You watch a TV screen to see what you are doing inside the abdomen with instruments that go through cannulas placed through the abdominal wall. Lap choles are probably the easiest laparoscopic procedures to learn because they are an easy procedure, and you do exactly the same thing you did with an open procedure. Other laparoscopic procedures are more involved. I decided to leave them to surgeons more expert than I. Now it seems they try to do everything laparoscopically.

Abdominal Surgery

Elderly patients can have a redundant distal colon that can twist on itself and cause what we call a sigmoid volvulus. It results in an obstruction of the bowel. Sometimes we can relieve the obstruction by untwisting the bowel using a proctoscope or colonoscope. Early on, we only had the proctoscope, essentially a rigid pipe. This was introduced into the rectum and slowly advanced into the colon. This was done with the patient lying on the left side. One could look through the instrument, but that required you to have your head on the bed so one eye could look into the pipe. This could be a dangerous position to be in because if you are successful in untwisting the bowel and relieving the obstruction, there is a sudden gush of bowel fluids that have been trapped above the obstruction. You have to move fast to get out of the way.

I had a nursing-home patient who repeatedly had a sigmoid volvulus. He was not a good candidate for a major operation. I thought if I could anchor the bowel by creating a colostomy it would prevent it from twisting again. I could create a colostomy under local anesthesia by simply bringing a loop of bowel out through a small incision and placing a glass rod under it. We were able to do this, and he tolerated it well. After going back to his room, however, he coughed, and the entire redundant bowel came out the small hole I had made. I decided if that was what the bowel wanted to do, then I would accommodate it. It's interesting that the wall of the bowel has no pain sensation to touch or heat, cutting or burning. It only has pain sensation with distension. The incision was still numb from local anesthetic, so I put in some sutures to secure the bowel to the abdominal wall and cut the redundant bowel away with cautery. He now had a double-barrel colostomy. I did this at the bedside, and he didn't feel a thing. He never had another volvulus.

A lady I see around town occasionally had a very interesting presentation. She said her husband could hear her bowel sounds from across the room. She also thought they were very loud. On work-up, we found a partial small bowel obstruction—a section of the small bowel was very narrow. When air or fluid is forced through a narrow area, it makes more noise. We did an exploration and found a tumor of the small bowel. We resected it, and pathology showed a lymphoma. She has not had any further disease.

I suspected a small bowel tumor in another patient but could never prove it. He presented with anemia—a low blood count. We did a complete work-up several times over the years but couldn't identify anything. He didn't want an exploratory lap. This was before laparoscopy was common. I wonder what we would have found if we had been able to look inside.

Twenty-five years ago, I did surgery on a gentleman from out of town. He presented with an acute abdomen, and we had to operate emergently. He had a perforated diverticulitis. I created a colostomy after washing all the fecal material out of his abdomen. He recovered well and went home. He is a cheese maker from eastern Wisconsin, and just recently, twenty-five years later, he sent me a box of cheese as a thank you.

I remember an elderly gentleman with rectal cancer whom I operated on. Post-op, when he was getting ready to go home, I was going over what he could and couldn't do. He asked if he could go fishing. I said, "As long as you don't go fishing for the big ones." He replied, "Have you ever gone fishing for the little ones?"

Another elderly gentleman on whom I had done an exploratory laparotomy was advised to do no lifting over twenty pounds for four weeks after he left the hospital. The next week, I saw him at the Monroe County Fair. He was showing his percherons, large black work horses. They had big heavy harnesses with silver decorations. I confronted him and asked, "Are you pushing those horses around and lifting those harnesses?" He said, "No, I have someone else doing that." As I was walking away, I heard him tell his friend, "That's the lady that cut on me!"

I cared for a forty-nine-year-old male with metastatic colon cancer. When it was diagnosed, it was unresectable. It was causing a very high bowel obstruction. Nothing could get beyond the stomach. He elected to receive IV hydration but no IV nutrition. He said he didn't want to feed the tumor. He had a gastrostomy so he could eat and drink, but it all came right back out again through the gastrostomy tube. I made house calls to see him on my way to and from Hillsboro. He would have lab work drawn, and based on the electrolyte results, I would order the IV solutions. A company in Milwaukee would mix them up and ship them out. His wife would administer them. It was quite a system. We were able to accommodate his wishes and keep him comfortable until the end.

Another patient I remember from my first years in Sparta was another relatively young man with colon cancer. He was receiving chemotherapy. Every week he would come into the clinic for IV treatment. It could be very challenging to find a vein, but once the IV was in we would run in a drug that could kill him and follow that with another drug to rescue him. This went on for over a year.

He eventually succumbed to his disease. His wife sent me a note thanking me for always giving them hope.

A third man with colon cancer had another amazing story. We discovered his cancer on upper endoscopy. It had eroded into the upper small bowel. He went to the Mayo Clinic for his initial surgery. It is my understanding that he received intraoperative radiation treatment. That is not something that is done routinely. He was okay for a while but then developed a bowel obstruction. They told him that the cancer had recurred and there was nothing they could do. He elected to have an IV port put in so he could go on IV nutrition. He ran this solution at night while he slept so he could be free during the day. He developed an infection in an obstructed loop of bowel that couldn't be cleared up with antibiotics. A surgeon in La Crosse did an operation to try to drain the area. He took out a large mass of tissue because it was all stuck together and put the bowel back together as best he could. He didn't find any cancer. The patient continued on the IV nutrition. He would occasionally ask to be taken off of it for a week so he could go fishing with his sons in Canada. He had a standing prescription for antibiotics to treat episodes of infection in the bowel. He managed quite well. Basically he would come to the clinic and tell me what he needed. He lived a long time this way. I don't think he had recurrent cancer. I think his problem was scarring from the radiation.

I operated on a lady to remove a retroperitoneal sarcoma. I took out all the tumor I could find. It recurred. We operated again. Again it recurred. This is a typical course for sarcoma. She decided not to have any more surgery. She developed pain and was admitted to the hospital for IV morphine. Eventually she was on an IV drip of morphine to control the pain. She remained awake and alert. We increased the morphine as she needed it. About that same time, I saw a TV movie about a nurse who was fired because she had given a patient 30 mg of morphine IV based on a physician's verbal order and the patient had died. My patient was on 120 mg of morphine an hour. It impressed me how much my patient was tolerating.

Breast Cancer

Early in my career I did many breast biopsies and mastectomies. Then the system required that any patient with a palpable mass had to go to the breast center in La Crosse for a workup. Also any patient with an abnormal mammogram had to go to La Crosse. They began doing stereotactic breast biopsies. And then most patients stayed in La Crosse for their surgery. They did breast conserving surgery and sentinel lymph node biopsies. As a result, I did fewer and fewer breast surgeries. The only patients I would see toward the end of my career were women with large breast masses. I did a needle biopsy on the mass to confirm the diagnosis and then did a mastectomy.

Several patients come to mind as exceptional. One young woman had a nipple abnormality. We did a mammogram and found several questionable areas in both breasts. I biopsied all of them, and they were all cancer. We did bilateral mastectomies.

I did a radical mastectomy on a male patient for breast cancer. He wore a brace because of a severe back abnormality and the top of the brace rubbed his chest in that area. I don't know if that was related or not.

One woman had inflammatory breast cancer, not a good prognosis. She underwent chemotherapy before surgery to try to shrink the tumor. I removed a breast with a huge fibroadenoma in it. It was causing the patient to tilt to the side because it was so heavy. Another patient requested bilateral mastectomies as treatment for her breast cancer in one breast. I see her around town occasionally, and she is very happy with her results.

One patient presented with a large fungating tumor of the breast. She thought it had been caused by exposure to chemicals at work. We did her mastectomy. She needed chemotherapy, so an IV port was placed. The chemotherapy drug leaked out of the port at one treatment, and the tissue around it died, so they had to take it out. They left the wound open so it could heal from the inside out. When she returned to clinic to see me, the wound was full of maggots. Her home living conditions were not good. She eventually came to live at the nursing home. I visited her there. She appreciated all the care she got.

I must have done good breast operations because when my scrub nurse needed surgery for breast cancer, she asked me to do it. I considered that quite a compliment.

A Couple of Other Stories

One day a nursing-home patient was brought to the clinic because he refused to eat. They couldn't figure out why. They also noted that he had lost his upper dentures. We did a chest X-ray and discovered that his denture was in the back of his throat. Once I pulled it out, he wanted something to eat.

I was asked to see a patient with an abscess on her neck. She was Hispanic and didn't speak English. The history I got was the bump had been there for a while, and now it was red and tender. She had what appeared to be a large abscess above her collarbone on the right. I explained to her through an interpreter that we needed to put in some numbing medicine and make a small incision to drain the abscess. She appeared to understand, so we proceeded. We got a little pus out but not as much as I expected based on the size of the inflamed area. We sent a sample for culture. I then was gone for about a week.

When I returned, she was on my schedule to be seen again. While I was gone the wound had closed over and one of the family practice physicians had opened it up again, but it wasn't getting any better. The culture we had sent was negative. It appeared that the wound was closed again and that I needed to make a bigger incision. The patient agreed with that approach. I made a much larger incision. Again I didn't get much pus, but I could see that the underlying tissue didn't appear normal. It looked smooth and white. I was reluctant to cut much deeper because we were right over the carotid artery and jugular vein. I did scrape away some tissue to see if we could get into another pocket of pus. I didn't get anything. I put the dressing on and sent the patient home.

As I was walking down the hall from the procedure room to my office, it occurred to me that the underlying tissue could be a "caseating granuloma," typical of TB. I had learned about this in medical school but had never seen it. I went back to the surgery room and retrieved all the sponges I had used to see if I could retrieve any of that white tissue to culture for TB. I notified the family practice doctor of what I suspected. He determined that since she wasn't coughing, she probably wasn't contagious. I then needed to contact the OB provider. Oh, I forgot to mention she was pregnant and due any day. It was Good Friday afternoon, and if she delivered over the weekend they would have had to have her in a negative pressure room. We called the patient back and did a chest X-ray. We didn't see any lesions in the lungs, but she did appear to have mediastinal masses. She probably didn't have pulmonary TB. After delivery, she was started on medications for TB. She reported feeling better shortly thereafter. She shared that she had felt so bad she thought she was going to die. Cultures came back positive for TB. That was the one and only case of TB I saw during my career.

18

The Least Expensive Carpal Tunnel Release

I have always done carpal tunnel releases under local anesthesia. I learned how to do them that way during my rotation on neurosurgery as a resident. Initially, I did them in the operating room. Then one day I asked myself why I was doing them there. I wasn't using anesthesia services, and I could create a sterile environment in the clinic for the procedure. I consulted the nurses in the clinic to see if they had any concerns or suggestions. They agreed to assist me, and thereafter I started doing them in the clinic. I actually had a patient come to me because he had shopped around and found that I had the cheapest carpal tunnel release in the state.

For those of you who aren't familiar with what a carpal tunnel release is, I will give you a little anatomy lesson and then describe the surgical procedure. Carpal tunnel syndrome is the most common nerve entrapment disorder. It is caused by increased pressure and consequent compression of the median nerve within the anatomic area referred to as the carpal tunnel. The carpal tunnel is the space between the wrist bones at the top of the wrist and a very thick band of tissue across the heel of the hand. The bones and the band of tissue create a rigid boundary to this space.

The median nerve is one of three nerves that provide sensation to the hand. If you look at the inside of your wrist, you will see a long tendon running right down the center toward your hand. The median nerve runs underneath this tendon. It goes through the carpal tunnel.

The muscles that allow us to flex our fingers and wrist are all in the forearm, and long tendons run down to the hand from these muscles. All these tendons go through the carpal tunnel. I usually tell patients that the purpose of the carpal tunnel is to keep in order and in place all these long tendons. Since the carpal tunnel has a rigid boundary, anything that takes up space in the tunnel puts pressure on the structures already there. This doesn't seem to bother the tendons, but it pinches the median nerve.

Many things can take up space in the carpal tunnel. The bones can get bigger due to trauma or fracture. The tendon sheaths can swell as in arthritis or overuse syndrome. The soft tissue can swell with edema as in pregnancy. Tumors can occur there. And systemic conditions, such as diabetes mellitus, thyroid dysfunction, amyloidosis, and Raynaud's disease, can be associated with carpal tunnel syndrome.

Patients usually present complaining of their hand going to sleep while driving or writing or using the computer. They may complain of waking up at night because their hand is numb or hurts and they have to shake it to wake it up. They may notice a weakness in the hand or that they are dropping things. They may have pain up into the forearm or even into the shoulder. Sometimes their only complaint is that their hand is numb.

I usually ask the patient what part of their hand goes to sleep or is numb. Since the median nerve provides sensation to the first three-and-a-half fingers of the hand, the patient usually says the thumb, index, and middle fingers. If the patient includes the little finger, there is involvement of the ulnar nerve, and that is a different syndrome.

When examining the patient, I look for muscle loss at the base of the thumb. The only motor branch of the median nerve goes to the muscle at the base of the thumb. Muscle loss is a late sign, but muscle weakness may be evident. That is tested by asking the patient to pinch the thumb and index finger together and then trying to pull them apart. A patient can have similar symptoms from a pinched nerve in the neck. A nerve conduction test is usually performed to confirm the diagnosis of carpal tunnel syndrome. It is not good to do a carpal tunnel release and not have relief of the symptoms because the problem was in the neck.

Surgical treatment of carpal tunnel syndrome relieves the pressure on the median nerve by cutting the thick band of tissue at the heel of the hand and allowing the carpal tunnel space to get bigger, thus giving the nerve more room. The procedure usually takes about fifteen minutes. As I do it under local anesthesia, the patient is awake and talking to me. The patient's arm is out on an arm board and is prepped and draped, just as in the operating room. I wear a mask, gown, and gloves after scrubbing up.

The patient does feel the initial needle prick as I put in the local anesthetic, but after that, there is minimal discomfort. I make an incision along the creases of the heel of the hand and the wrist. After healing, it is sometimes difficult to see the incision. I extend the incision into the deeper tissues at the heel of the hand until I encounter that thick band of tissue. It can be very hard to cut. Once I have cut through it in one small place, I can usually see a structure underneath. I then ask the patient to make a fist. If what I am looking at under the band is a tendon, it will move. If it is the nerve, it doesn't. Once I am convinced I am over the nerve, I slip a scissors in to cut the band of tissue toward the fingers and toward the forearm to completely disrupt it. I stay on top of the nerve because the motor branch to the muscle at the base of the thumb comes off of the side of the nerve, and I don't want to cut that. After I have completely cut the band of tissue, I ask the patient to touch the tip of the little finger to the tip of the thumb. This tells me the motor branch still works.

The skin is the only layer that is stitched closed. A dressing is applied, and a wrist splint is put in place. I require the patient to leave everything in place as I have put it for two days. Then the patient can remove the splint and dressing and bathe. The splint should be replaced and worn at all times except for bathing until the patient returns in ten days for suture removal. The hand should stay elevated over the level of the heart for the rest of the day of surgery to reduce swelling. Whatever the patient normally takes for a headache can be used to manage any discomfort. If the patient keeps the hand elevated, there is usually very little discomfort.

After ten days, the patient is allowed to use the hand normally, but anything that puts pressure on the incision requires use of the splint during that activity. That restriction is in place for two months. Most patients do very well. Carpal tunnel syndrome can recur if a patient returns to the activity that caused it in the first place. A release can be redone. I have done several patients more than once. I have done four procedures on the same hand of one patient.

With all the talk about the cost of health care, I recently wondered how much money I have saved my patients by doing their procedures under local anesthesia in the clinic. My charge was the same, but there was no hospital or anesthesia charge. I figured out how many of these procedures I had done: 435. The hospital charge for the procedure is $4,200. When you multiply that out, you find that my clinic procedure results in a savings of nearly two million dollars.

I made a presentation at the Wisconsin Surgical Society meeting in November 2010 about how I do carpal tunnel releases. I suggested that maybe others would consider doing them the same way. It costs less and does not compromise patient care.

19

On Call

For the first thirteen years in Sparta, I was the only surgeon in town. For the first ten years, I was on call every day, twenty-four/seven, unless I left town. If I was going to be gone, I would arrange for another rural surgeon to cover for me, usually the surgeon in Mauston, fifty miles away. It was several years before I met the surgeon in Mauston. We covered for each other but were never in the same place at the same time.

After my divorce in 1988, I was a single mom of a two-year-old and on call all the time.

In 1992, when we affiliated with Gundersen Lutheran, I started to share call with the surgeon in Tomah who was also affiliated with Gundersen Lutheran. When on call, we covered Tomah, Sparta, and Hillsboro. We covered our own communities during the week and shared the weekend call. I was off every other weekend!

Other surrounding communities had their own surgeons, and occasionally I would be asked to cover for them. There were several weekends when I would cover more than three hospitals. And then there was one weekend in 1993 when I was on call for six different communities all on the same weekend—Sparta, Tomah, Black River Falls, Viroqua, Mauston, and Hillsboro. I was only covering for

C-sections. A hospital could not deliver babies unless they had a surgeon on call for a possible C-section. Luckily, I didn't get called by any of them that weekend. I have never been needed for an emergency in more than one hospital at the same time despite the fact that I covered more than one a lot of times. I do recall I had to delay an appendectomy once to do an emergency C-section at another hospital. After the C-section, I went back to the first hospital and did the appendectomy. After my malpractice jury trial in 2000, I didn't cover more than two hospitals at a time.

I can recall only one time when I went to the wrong hospital when I was called. After that I made sure I knew who was calling me. They had to identify the hospital because there was at least one nurse who worked in the ER of more than one hospital and so if I recognized his voice I still couldn't tell which hospital was calling.

When FSH affiliated with the Mayo Clinic in 1995, they said they were going to hire their own surgeon for Sparta and Tomah. They did in 1996.

Eventually the three surgeons—myself, the surgeon in Tomah, and the Sparta Mayo surgeon—shared call coverage for Tomah, Sparta, and Hillsboro. For two years, I was on call every third weekend! This was great!

In July 2000, the surgeon in Tomah retired. I told Gundersen Lutheran I would provide surgical call coverage and do clinic hours in Tomah until they could find another surgeon. I was also going to Hillsboro once a week. By August, I stopped providing services in Hillsboro. I was burning out and had to eliminate something.

Then in December 2001, the Mayo surgeon, who was in the Air Force reserves, got called up to serve in Iraq. Now I found myself as the only surgeon on call for both Sparta and Tomah. I was back to being on call twenty-four/seven, but now I was covering two communities! After three months FSH/Mayo was able to find a locum tenens surgeon to help out. Locums were short-term, though, so we had to continually look for others. It was hard to find locum tenens general surgeons who did C-sections. The locums would stay for anywhere from a week to three months. Several of them did several stints, and I got to know them well. They were all good surgeons. One had worked in Sparta for about a year in the '70s.

The surgeon in the reserves was gone the first time for six-and-a-half months and then returned for ten months. Then he left again for six months and was back for four months. Then he was gone for a year, during which time he wasn't doing surgery. When he returned, it was proposed that he do some training to bring him back up to speed. He resigned soon afterward, and it is my understanding that he went into the service full-time.

From 2000 to 2007 Gundersen Lutheran, FSH/Mayo, and the Tomah Hospital were all recruiting for a surgeon without success. The locum tenens surgeons came and went. It got harder and harder to find surgeons to help short-term. Then a female surgeon was hired for three months. I was excited. After a month, I began to hear comments from the OR crew about "him." I am very trusting and naive. I accepted her for who she said she was. Then I found out that she was a he. Okay. Then I reflected on what had been happening. Several times I had been changing clothes in the locker room with her. She tended to stand and watch rather than change her clothes too. Now I felt violated. Administration apparently knew that her license was issued to a male, but she had made them promise not to tell anyone. So I felt let down by administration.

If the gender issue is no big deal, just natural, as cross-gender people claim, why not say so up front? I don't think I would have treated her any differently if I had known. But I would have changed clothes in the bathroom. The way it happened, it became a big deal. As it turned out, she had problems with her laparoscopic cholecystectomies, and the hospital asked me to scrub with her on those cases, so that added to my responsibilities rather than helping me out.

I was getting tired. I asked the family practice doctors to do the initial evaluations on ER patients before calling me. I asked them to do the pre-op histories and physicals. When I got really tired, I would only cover for C-sections. All general surgery patients could be transported to La Crosse.

In January 2006, I stopped covering for Sparta. I couldn't do it all anymore. I was on call for the Tomah clinic patients all the time, twenty-four/seven, except for an occasional weekend when Gundersen Lutheran would pay one of the other rural surgeons to cover for me from Saturday morning until Sunday night. Looking at the call schedule for that year and the next, my name is the only one on it.

With more patients suing their physicians, OB providers became less willing to have a surgeon covering more than one hospital at a time. They wanted to know where I was at all times in case they needed me. The Tomah providers wanted me to inform them if I was scrubbed on a case in Sparta, etc.

I rarely got sick. But in 2004, I developed bronchospasm. I didn't have a history of asthma, but I found I couldn't breathe well. I recognized it because I couldn't sing in church. I had my husband take me to the ER. They made the diagnosis and put me on medication. They told me I had to take two days off. That shut down the OB units in two hospitals. They couldn't do deliveries without a surgeon available to do a C-section. There was no other surgeon.

In October 2007, the Tomah Hospital hired a part-time surgeon, but he didn't do C-sections. He was willing to learn. He lives in Pennsylvania and comes to Tomah every other week.

In November 2007, Gundersen Lutheran was able to hire a surgeon for their clinic in Tomah. He could do C-sections.

In January 2008, the Sparta Hospital stopped providing OB services.

In February 2008, FSH/Mayo hired a surgeon for their Tomah and Sparta clinics. He also did C-sections.

Three additional surgeons were now helping me provide surgical coverage for Sparta and Tomah.

In December 2008, the Sparta Hospital stopped doing after-hours surgery.

I was back to three-way call and only covering one hospital, Tomah. We would take turns covering C-sections when the hospital surgeon was on call. I began thinking of getting off call. I thought I had done my share.

It had been my understanding for years that at Gundersen Lutheran, when you were fifty-five years old, you could go off call. Sometime during the surgeon recruitment process, I learned that that was not the case. Apparently early in 2005, the surgery department of Gundersen Lutheran had decided that regardless of your age, if you went off call, after a year you had to either retire or return to taking call. When I heard that, I was very upset. I was supposed to be part of the surgery department. I had not been asked for input on the issue. I had not been asked to help make the decision. And I had not been informed that the decision had been made. Their excuse for not letting me know was they had no idea anyone in the region was near that age.

I made a very emotional appeal to the executive committee. I was tired. I wanted to go off call, but I wanted to continue to work in the clinic for ten more years. The answer was no. So I continued to take call.

I was seeing patients in the Sparta clinic, but I wasn't very busy. They needed a surgeon to provide endoscopy and surgical services at the Tri-County Memorial Hospital in Whitehall. So in January 2009, I started going to Whitehall one day a week. I mostly did colonoscopies with a few surgical cases—lap choles, carpal tunnel releases, and hernias. I liked this outreach. I had done a similar schedule in Black River Falls when they were without a surgeon in the late '90s.

I finally did go off of call January 1, 2009. They allowed me to continue with a clinic and surgery practice for two years before I retired. So I retired January 1, 2011. I was sixty years old.

The first year I was off surgery call, I was essentially on call for my mother. She lived with us and had ovarian cancer and was slowly dwindling. She passed away in December 2009.

I have been enjoying being off call and doing things when I want to do them. When I was on call, I always had to consider what to do if I were to get called away whenever I planned to do something. I remember one time I left my husband and son at the movie theater because I got called. Someone gave them a ride home.

I think the most restrictive thing was that I felt tethered and thought I couldn't go much of anywhere. I had to be within a twenty-minute range of the hospital. I did gardening and read a lot of books. I was very active in the Christian school and in my church. In retrospect, I don't think I missed out on anything because I was on call. I was on call a lot of time, but I wasn't always called.

I can remember only one weekend when I was overwhelmingly busy. It was in the early '80s, and it happened to be a weekend when my husband's father and stepmom were visiting. I don't think I spent more than an hour with them. By Sunday evening, I was so tired I didn't trust my judgment anymore. I asked one of the older family practice doctors to see a patient with me to make sure I wasn't missing something.

In 2005, we did a golf fundraiser for the Christian school. I had never golfed before, but I discovered I enjoyed it and could do it pretty well. I decided to take lessons. I then discovered that the Sparta golf course is set up so that while you are on the course, you are never very far from the clubhouse and parking lot. If I rented a golf cart, I could get back to my car and get to where I needed to be within the required time frame. As I began to play the game, I discovered that I could actually forget I was on call while I was golfing. That was really something. I can't think of anything else I ever did that allowed me to forget I was on call. And I loved being out of doors, especially early in the morning. So I began golfing regularly.

Speaking of not being able to forget I was on call, I remember one time when my parents were traveling and my mom got diarrhea and was hospitalized in Nebraska. She asked her physician to call me. When I answered the phone and the physician identified himself and told me where he was calling from, my first thought was, *I'm not covering Nebraska.*

When I met my second husband, our courtship was interesting. I had to call the hospital and tell them where I was or that I was going to be on the beeper. They knew where I was and what I was doing all the time. It would be interesting to get my husband's and son's perspective on how my being on call affected their lives.

Surgery has changed a lot in the last thirty years. Being on call isn't what it used to be. Ideally you should have someone to share call with so you have some time of your own. But some of the best cases come in when you are on call, the ones that challenge you and give you the most satisfaction. I wouldn't have wanted to miss those. There has to be a balance in there somewhere.

Between 2001 and 2007, I was willing to do what I did because I was, in a way, serving my country. I was just doing it at home.

When I retired from the Gundersen Lutheran Sparta Clinic in January 2011, they did not replace me. All surgery done in Sparta now is elective and done by either outreach surgeons from La Crosse or the FSH surgeon from Tomah. I was the last surgeon who lived in Sparta.

20

Being a Rural Surgeon

Having grown up in a rural community, I always thought I would live in a rural community. I knew I didn't like big city life after being exposed to it during medical school and residency. So I only looked for a place to practice that was in a small rural community. As you'll remember, that's how I ended up in Sparta.

There are multiple benefits to practicing surgery in a small town. Since I was the only surgeon in town, I could schedule my cases whenever I wanted. Being only thirty miles from two large medical institutions, I could be selective about the kinds of surgery I wanted to do and the cases I took on. I worked with the same surgery crew every day. We knew each other well and what we each could do. We all wanted to do our cases well so people would choose to have their surgery done in Sparta rather than in La Crosse.

I did a wide variety of surgeries, and I wore many hats in the OR. I could help set up the sterile instruments. I could help transport the patient. I helped the anesthetist put the patient to sleep or put in the spinal. I helped move the patient off the table, onto the cart, and into the recovery room. I even sometimes helped transport the patient to the med/surg floor from the recovery room. I knew the whole process intimately.

One of the surgeons from La Crosse came to Sparta to assist me on several laparoscopic cholecystectomies after I had the common bile duct injury in 1993. On one of those cases, the anesthetist was unable to intubate the patient. I stepped to the head of the OR table and intubated the patient, and then we continued with the procedure. That must have really impressed the surgeon from La Crosse, because he shared that story with all the surgeons at a special surgery department meeting I attended.

There were only two grocery stores in town. It was not uncommon for me to see people on whom I had performed surgery when I was grocery shopping. Sometimes they would approach me and lift up their shirt to show me their scars. Sometimes I would recognize the scar before I would recognize the patient. It may have been that I had only seen the patient in a hospital gown, their hair all messed up, lying in bed. My husband would know when I didn't remember the patient. I was always cordial, but he could tell. Some people seemed to be surprised that I had to grocery shop. How else was I supposed to get food?

Eventually, I would more often than not know the family of a patient who presented for a surgical consult. I also had many patients return for other surgical procedures. Many patients were referred by other patients I had operated on. And living in the small community, I interacted socially with patients. I got to know some of my patients personally.

One of the things that disappointed me the most was that some patients assumed that "bigger was better." Even though I had the same training, credentials, and experience as the surgeons in La Crosse, patients would either not come to the clinic in Sparta at all or when they learned that they would need surgery, they would ask to be transferred to La Crosse. I would always accommodate their request, but I think I could have done their procedure just as well.

Studies have been published that try to show that hospitals that do a lot of a particular procedure have better outcomes. I agree that could be true for some procedures, such as open-heart surgery or Whipple procedures, but I don't think it applies to all major procedures. These articles tend to direct patients to the larger hospitals for surgery. I could never understand why they didn't think we were capable of doing the procedure, but when a patient had gone home from the big hospital and had a complication, then we were suddenly good enough because the patient didn't want to go all the way back to La Crosse.

The type of surgery I did in Sparta was not necessarily limited by what I was capable of doing. It also was limited by what the nurses and other support staff were familiar with. I didn't think it reasonable to expect the nurses to be comfortable caring for a patient post-op who'd had a major surgery when they hadn't cared for such a patient in over a year. As time went on, we did less and less major surgery, so they had less and less experience caring for those kinds of patients. Also, as laparoscopic surgery was used for more procedures, we did less of the major open surgeries. My practice became about 50 percent scoping procedures.

One day I realized that I was the only one who knew my entire schedule. Each OR knew what cases were scheduled at its hospital. Each clinic knew when I was scheduled to see patients at its facility. They also had a general idea of when I was scheduled in another clinic or hospital, but they didn't know whom I was operating on. My little black book was the only place where it was all written down in one place.

I remember I called Gundersen Clinic in La Crosse one time for information on a patient. They stated that they would have to look it up and get back to me. They asked if they should call me back or call my secretary. What secretary?

Another time I called the gastrointestinal lab in La Crosse for information on how to fix the post-op report computer program. They were going to call me back and wondered if they should ask for the GI lab. I told them to just call the hospital and ask for me. I was the GI lab that day. I handled my own phone calls and did the troubleshooting on the equipment myself. There just wasn't anyone else.

One of the hardest things for me to do was to determine if I was too ill to operate. Occasionally I suffered from severe headaches and sinus infections. I would get sick to my stomach when I had a headache, so I couldn't take any oral medication. If I took a pill, it would come right back up. If I vomited and then slept, the headache would go away, but I didn't always have time to do that. I recall at least two procedures I did with a bad headache. I was amazed that during the procedure the headache was gone, probably because my adrenaline level was high. As soon as I was done, the headache came back. The morning after my fiftieth birthday party, I ended up in the ER for a hypo to get rid of a headache. I then learned of a pill for migraine headaches that dissolves under your tongue. I didn't have to swallow it. I got some of those pills and carried them in my purse. I never had a severe headache after that. Just having the medication available apparently cured my headaches.

Once I had gotten my feet wet in Sparta, I began to look for some surgical comaraderie in the area. All the surgeons were in similar situations to mine and were busy. We shared call occasionally, but we actually seldom met.

To meet my continuing medical education needs, I initially attended the annual University of Minnesota Surgery Conference. I found that all the presentations were given by academic surgeons, and they all seemed to be saying, "Look at the great things I am doing." They weren't sharing any ideas that I could incorporate into my practice.

In 1990, on the recommendation of a surgeon I had gone to residency with, I decided to go to the Current Topics in General Surgery conference in Dallas, Texas. The course is sponsored by the University of Texas and held at the Southwestern Medical Center. Their presentations were more of, "This is the way I do things. Maybe you could use this in your practice." I found it to be more applicable to what I did. I went to that conference for several years.

In 1999, I returned to the University of Minnesota Surgery Conference basically because I was tired of traveling to Texas. Their focus had changed and become similar to that of the Dallas Conference. I would learn things I could apply to my own practice.

I sought membership in the Wisconsin Surgical Society and the Wisconsin Chapter of the American College of Surgeons to be able to talk to other surgeons and share interesting cases. The reality was, however, that those meetings were dominated by surgeons from large metropolitan areas. All the presentations were about surgical cases and issues in academic programs. It didn't pertain to what I was doing. The other surgeons in my area were not members of these societies.

I became a charter member of the American Society of General Surgeons, again hoping to find comaraderie with other rural surgeons. I attended the first meeting in Philadelphia, Pennsylvania. But again the emphasis seemed to focus on academic, institutional surgery. The society had formed because surgical specialties were beginning to limit the scope of general surgery practice. There were now breast surgeons, colorectal surgeons, hernia surgeons, vascular surgeons, thoracic surgeons, laparoscopic surgeons, and others.

When we affiliated with Gundersen Lutheran in 1990, I automatically became part of the surgery department. All the rural surgeons were considered part of the department. We were invited to attend surgery department meetings and grand rounds, but when you are the only surgeon in town, you tend not to leave very often. I would have to find call coverage in order to go. So I wasn't seen there very much, and my needs and concerns were not presented very frequently.

In 1996, six other rural surgeons and I were invited to contribute to a study that attempted to define the types of surgery performed by rural surgeons. I was asked to compile a list of procedures I performed, the outcomes, and morbidity and mortality. The results were published in the *Archives of Surgery Journal* in 1997. The lead author of the article was a surgeon from Gundersen Lutheran in

La Crosse. The conclusion was that a large volume of surgery was performed with low mortality by seven rural general surgeons in the Gundersen Lutheran system. Our operative experience differed from that of their 1995 surgery residency graduates. It was recommended that a rural surgical track in selected training programs be developed to prepare graduates better for rural practice. Since then, numerous articles have been written about the need for rural surgeons and the need for training programs for rural surgeons.

In 2003, I had the opportunity to visit Russia. I was invited to participate in a People to People Ambassador program with the Association of Women Surgeons. I was not a member of the association, but I got an invitation and liked to travel, so I decided to go. There were twenty-three women surgeons in the group. There were breast surgeons, plastic surgeons, an orthopedic surgeon, ob-gyn surgeons, a cardiothoracic surgeon, and one other general surgeon. She practiced in a surgical group practice in Ohio.

We visited Moscow and St. Petersburg. We did some sightseeing, but mostly we visited hospitals, research facilities, museums, and universities in both cities. At each institution, we would meet with local doctors and get a tour of the facility.

Before I went to Russia, it was my impression that most physicians there were women. But at our first encounter with Russian surgeons, the host said that he had never seen so many female surgeons in one place before. Apparently most primary care physicians were female, such as family practice, pediatrics, etc. They were not paid well enough to support a family. Most specialists were male.

At each facility, we would introduce ourselves, say where we were from, and share what kind of surgery we did. I would say, "I am Judy Lottmann. I am from a small rural community in Wisconsin. I am the surgeon in town."

The last facility we visited was the Pavlov State Medical University in St. Petersburg. We met with the surgical staff, the residents, and the medical students in a small amphitheater. After our introduction, we had a lively discussion via interpreters about surgery in general. Finally, our leader asked the head of the surgery department if he had any questions for us. He asked, "What kind of surgery do you do in small rural communities?" Everyone in our group turned to me. I said, "I do hernia repairs, appendectomies, breast surgery, gallbladder removals, C-sections, bowel resections, and other abdominal surgeries." That seemed to answer his question.

As we got on the bus to leave, other surgeons in our group turned to me and asked, "You do C-sections?" I said, "Yes." Then they asked, "What do the ob-gyn docs do?" I replied, "There are no ob-gyn surgeons. I am *the* surgeon in town."

I had been saying the same thing throughout the trip, but it apparently hadn't registered that I was the *only* surgical person in town. What amazed me was that the women surgeons from America didn't understand what kind of practice I had as a rural surgeon!

In 2004, I was invited to participate in a summer research project examining rural medical practice. The University of Wisconsin School of Medicine and Public Health wanted to learn more about what factors and issues resulted in women physicians entering medical practice in rural Wisconsin. They interviewed ten female physicians practicing in rural Wisconsin. The study resulted in an article in a 2007 issue of the *Wisconsin Medical Journal*. The conclusion was that female physicians find that the value of being in rural practice overcomes the challenges. It sought to provide insight into motivating women to enter rural practice.

In 2004, I went to the American College of Surgeons Meeting in New Orleans. I attended a forum on rural surgery. It was an opportunity for rural surgeons to bring their concerns to the leaders of the American College of Surgeons. That was the first I had heard that the American College of Surgeons was interested in the concerns of rural surgeons.

In 2005, I was excited to hear there was going to be a rural surgery symposium sponsored by the Mithoefer Center for Rural Surgery in

Cooperstown, New York, in May. Here was an opportunity to share with other rural surgeons. I registered right away and attended the symposium. I returned to Cooperstown in September 2006 to attend the Second Annual Rural Surgery Symposium. And I attended the third in Grand Forks, North Dakota, in 2007. Here were surgeons who spoke to my needs and concerns. They also addressed the future surgical needs of rural communities.

The American College of Surgeons also began to address the unique needs of rural surgeons. In the July 2009 issue of the *Bulletin of the American College of Surgeons*, I learned that the college's online portal had a rural surgeons' community. It provides links to the most recent journal articles related to surgery in rural areas. It also has a link to a rural surgeons' discussion forum and has created the rural surgeons' network. This makes connecting with other rural surgeons only a click away.

The Fifth Annual Rural Surgery Symposium was held May 2011 at the American College of Surgeons headquarters in Chicago.

The February 2012 edition of *Selected Readings in General Surgery* published by the American College of Surgeons was dedicated to rural surgery. And the Board of Regents of the American College of Surgeons established the ACS Advisory Council for Rural Surgery in June 2012. This is the only new advisory council they have created in the past fifty years.

When I applied for membership in the various surgical organizations or for hospital staff privileges, the most difficult section to complete on the application was the reference section. They wanted someone who knew me and my surgical competence well enough to write a reference, preferably a surgeon. I didn't work closely with any other surgeon. Usually I would get one of the family practice physicians to write the reference.

When a physician initially acquires hospital medical staff privileges, they are probationary privileges for the first several months. Another physician on the medical staff is asked to proctor the new physician to assess his or her level of competence before the physician is given full privileges. Since I was the only surgeon on staff when the three new surgeons came on board in Tomah, I was asked to proctor them. Having been the only surgeon in town, we did things in the OR and the hospital the way I wanted to do them. I believed the way I did things was the best way. I had assumed that all surgeons did things much the same way I did. In proctoring the other surgeons, I discovered that that wasn't the case. Other surgeons did some things differently.

Early in 2011, I received an invitation to a reception for women surgeons to be held at the home of the chairman of the department of surgery of the University of Wisconsin in Madison. I was surprised to receive the invitation. I had not gotten one before, and I assumed this was not the first reception they had had for women surgeons.

I e-mailed the organizer of the event and asked her what it was about and why I was invited. She said they had held a couple of receptions before but had only invited women surgeons from Madison and Milwaukee. They also included female surgical residents and students. In 2011 they decided to invite women surgeons from other institutions in the state. I was invited because I was a part of Gundersen Lutheran. I wonder if they miss women surgeons who practice independently or in small groups.

I decided to go to the reception. It was a very nice event. There were many women there, approximately sixty. I had never seen so many women surgeons in one place. A woman surgeon from St. Louis had also been invited. She was scheduled to speak at Grand Rounds the next day.

As we gathered in the living room, residents and students were encouraged to ask questions. One resident asked if surgery ever got boring. No one responded right away, so I spoke up. I said, "No, it doesn't get boring. You may do the same procedure multiple times, but no two patients are exactly the same. The anatomy can be different, there may be other pathology, there may be adhesions from a previous procedure, instruments may be different, and the people you are working with may be different. Also, it doesn't get boring because surgery is a natural high."

Then the guest surgeon responded. She said, "No, it doesn't get boring because you try to do every operation better that you did the last one. You study the situation and plan your approach."

I have reflected on our different responses. As a specialized surgeon, she was coming from a perspective of having a multitude of scans to study and days to plan her operation. Where I was, I did what had to be done when it had to be done. The majority of my cases were common ones, and a large percentage of them were urgent or emergent. I didn't spend days studying and planning many of them. This is one of the differences between rural surgeons and university/academic surgeons.

I am aware that there is currently a shortage of general surgeons and particularly rural surgeons in this country. During the last several years of my practice, I would receive four to five recruitment letters a week for a general surgeon. Even though I am retired, I still receive an occasional recruitment letter. Twice during my first two years of retirement, the local hospital called to ask if I would be willing to cover for surgery for a weekend. They didn't have a surgeon available.

One of the reasons I retired when I did was because I wanted to retire when I was still doing a good job. I didn't want to be forced out because of a mistake or a bad outcome. I could sense that my skills were not as good as they used to be. I didn't agree to provide surgical coverage for the hospital because what they needed was C-section coverage so they could deliver babies. Being on call for C-sections is the most serious thing I did. I would be called to do surgery emergently on two patients, and the situation was usually critical. I hadn't done surgery for a while, and I think I would have been putting the patients at risk. I discovered that even though I still loved doing the surgery, I was burnt out on being responsible for the patient.

Part of living in a rural area is you don't have easy access to cultural activities, such as the opera and the ballet. On the trip to Russia in 2003, I attended the ballet and the symphony for the first time.

One of my biggest concerns about the trip to Russia was whether I had the appropriate clothes to wear. I took some basic black outfits, and my roommate helped me with accessories. I did okay. But just to give you an idea of my understanding of appropriate attire, I have to tell you a story.

St. Paul Ramsey held a twentieth-year residency reunion and tribute to Dr. Perry in May 2001. It was to be held at the St. Paul University Club. The invitation read "black tie optional." That told my husband what to wear, but it didn't tell me anything. It was spring, so I wore a two-piece blue-and-white-flower ensemble with white shoes. When we arrived, we were surprised at the elegance of the event. There was a valet service to park the car. We were a bit early. As other people arrived, it became obvious that I was dressed inappropriately. Every other woman was in either a black or navy blue evening gown. I didn't own such a gown. As the reception progressed, I tried to be inconspicuous by standing against the wall. My husband was with me. He usually isn't comfortable at these kinds of events anyway. As we were standing there, it occurred to me how funny the situation was. I turned to my husband and said, "What would you say if I told you that my shoe was being held together with duct tape?" It was true. I had bought the shoes at Walmart, and the inside of one had cracked, so I had put a piece of duct tape in it.

At the dinner, my plan was to sit as out of sight as possible, but they had tables reserved for the residents at the front of the room. The organizers of the event presented each resident with one of Dr. Perry's original teaching slides. We had to go to the podium to accept the gift. So much for my being inconspicuous! No one commented on my outfit. They were very kind.

Multiple people spoke in tribute to Dr. Perry. They told how he treated everyone equally with respect—from housekeepers to nurses to residents to colleagues. It made me reflect on what had attracted me to this residency. I had thought it was because of all the women in the program. Now I think it may have been more of the way his attitude set the tone for the entire surgery department.

One comment about the electronic medical record: I wonder if anyone took into consideration how it would affect a physician who worked in several different hospitals and clinics. Usually physicians work in two facilities, their clinic and hospital, and they may have the same electronic medical record. But usually each facility has its own version of the electronic medical record, and they don't all work the same. In order to work in the various medical facilities, I found myself dealing with multiple systems. Even though I could use the same password, they all used a different thought process. I frequently needed help navigating a system to get my work done and recorded. I retired as they were changing the program in the Gundersen Lutheran System. I decided not to invest the time and energy into learning another system before I left.

Over the last couple of weeks, I've encountered an interesting phenomenon. One day I was helping plant cranberries, and there was another lady there who I didn't know. I went over to introduce myself. I said, "Hello. I don't think I've met you. My name is Judy." She said, "I'm Marsha. You delivered my firstborn nineteen years ago." Two days later, when visiting a friend at the Hospice House, I went to the nurse's station to ask a question. The nurse said, "Are you a sister?" I said, "No, I'm Dr. Lottmann." She said, "Oh yes. You took out my son's appendix."

Three days later, my husband and I were at a funeral. I was sitting next to one of the nurses from the hospital. She introduced me to some friends of hers, a couple sitting in the row in front of us. The man turned around and said, "You took out my gallbladder. No one else could figure out what was wrong with me. But you said it was my gallbladder and took it out, and I haven't had a problem since." Then his wife turned around and said, "You took mine out, too." I said, "I've left my mark on a lot of people." I hadn't encountered so many people in such a short amount of time that I had operated on. I took it as a sign that I was supposed to include it in this book.

21

Being a Female Surgeon

I don't believe being a female surgeon is any different from being a male surgeon. I have not become a member of any society that is exclusively for female surgeons. The reason for this may be the fact that there were not many female surgeons when I became one, let alone societies of women surgeons. But I didn't have to deal with tenure, promotion, or a position in the department, either. As I have said earlier, I consider myself a child of God first, a wife second, a mother third, and then I am a surgeon. I got the support I needed from family and my church family more than from any medical or surgical society.

I did struggle with what my role as a wife was. My income was always greater than my husband's, and he sacrificed a lot to be my husband. As a Christian wife, I am to submit to my husband. I don't have any problem with that. In fact, he is very wise and has helped me make some very difficult decisions. Some think there are specific things that need to be done around the house that are the wife's responsibility. But there were times when I was not home a lot, so what was my role?

After much prayer, soul searching, research, and reading, I concluded that my role as a wife is to be a "help mate," to come alongside my husband and help him. I usually say my responsibility is "to make him look good." To me that means listen to him, help him do what he likes to do, never speak negatively about him, encourage him, respect him, and esteem him above all others. You'll notice none of that says who is responsible for what around the house. In our situation, we both contributed to get the work done.

Early on, when I would meet new people they would ask what kind of work I did. I would usually say I worked at the hospital. If they asked further what I did there, then I would tell them I was a surgeon. Once they knew I was a surgeon, the conversation would either end or they would ask me a medical question. Being a surgeon didn't lend itself to making new friends with women.

I once had lunch with a classmate from high school whom I hadn't seen for a number of years. She had teenage children. I had basically been going to school since leaving high school. Other than high school, it seemed we didn't have anything in common anymore.

I think it is important that women have women friends. I was friends with a member of the OR crew and a couple of employees at the clinic. But it wasn't until I became a Christian that I established deep friendships with anyone outside the medical field. People at church accept me for who I am, not for what I do, and that's where I get my significance.

I anticipated that I would get some reluctance on the part of men to let me examine them for things like hernias or other problems in the genital area. It has surprised me over the years that I have never had a male patient have a problem with it. I approach the exam as a routine part of the assessment, and we just do it. I have had one female patient ask to see another surgeon. She wanted a male surgeon. I don't remember what her medical problem was.

I had gotten my medical license before I was married. I researched if I could change my professional name once I got married. I discovered that it would require signed affidavits from the chairman of the department of surgery where I did my residency and from two other surgeons. For me, that was a problem. The residency didn't exist anymore, and there were no surgeons who could speak on my behalf. So I decided to maintain my maiden name as my professional name and use my married name as my legal name. I was told that as long as I did this consistently, it would be okay. I maintained my social security number in my maiden name because that was the name on my paychecks. I used my married name on my driver's license, checkbook, and passport. This created interesting situations when I traveled overseas on medical trips, but it worked. Everything was fine until after the 9/11 attacks. When I went to renew my driver's license in 2004, I discovered that it had to be in the same name as my social security number. So they changed the name on my driver's license, and after developing my picture, they told me to sign the license. I asked them which name I should sign. They said to sign it like I sign my checks. So I signed my married name. So I had a printed name on my license that was not the same as the signed name. When I wrote a check and people asked to see my driver's license, no one ever commented on the difference. Since I have retired, I have changed my social security number to my married name, and I no longer have the discrepancy.

Since I have been married twice and have had a different professional name, people at church have found it very confusing to know which name to use, so they call me Dr. Judy.

22

Completing My Call

There is life after surgery!

I retired January 1, 2011. I had been a surgeon in Sparta for twenty-eight years. I was concerned that I wouldn't be busy enough after retiring, so I considered all sorts of possibilities of things I could do:

- I planned to read for two hours every morning. I love to read and have acquired a lot of books I haven't had the opportunity to read.
- I was going to write this book, so I would write for two hours every morning.
- I wanted to learn about how government worked and was considering running for a local office.
- I wanted to take Peacemaker training.
- I was interested in going on a mission trip.
- I am a facilitator for "The Truth Project" and wanted to share that information with others.
- I would perhaps finish my master's degree in bioethics.

- I was interested in being a patient advocate—going with people to their medical appointments and helping them through the medical system.

So what would I do?

I ran for the office of town clerk and was elected. Our town is small, about 137 residents. I do all the paperwork and keep track of all the money. I also am in charge of running the elections locally.

I enrolled in a course sponsored by the Christian Medical Society titled "Completing Your Call." It is a sixteen-month course, tailored to help physicians in midlife decide what God has for them to do now that they are credentialed and well established in their practices. I asked if it would be appropriate for me to take the course since I was retiring, and they said yes. The course involved reading books, writing brief book reports, teleconferencing with the authors of the books, and attending three weekend workshops at the home office in Bristol, Tennessee.

I thoroughly enjoyed the course. I remembered that I had had so much schooling because I liked to go to school. And here I was essentially going to school again. I like to read and learn and share, and that was what I was doing. We read books for the course that I have wanted to read for a long time and others that I never knew existed but that were a great help in understanding myself.

I was reminded that we are made up of three components—spiritual, intellectual, and physical. I have ignored the physical aspect for most of my life. I am trying to address that now.

Part of the course was "Discovering Your Design." I learned that my skills and talents are as follows:

- I am a team player.
- I can be a leader if I know where we are going. I am not a visionary.
- I pay attention to detail.
- I want to get the job done.

- I want to do the job right.
- I like to organize things and keep them in order.
- I am a problem solver.
- I like to work with numbers.
- I like to learn and share what I am learning.

In reflecting on my career as a rural surgeon, all of these skills and talents match the requirements to do well in that setting. God had put me in a position that matched the way he had made me. I find it very interesting that these same skills and talents match being the town clerk. I really enjoy that job as well.

I think it is great that I have learned this about myself, but I think this kind of exercise should be done when you are a teenager or young adult so you can use this information to choose an occupation that matches your skills and talents.

One medically affiliated activity I still do is as a member of the Ethics Committee at the local hospital. I also attend a quarterly ethics roundtable sponsored by the Wisconsin Rural Hospital Association. I continue to attend the Bioethics Conference at Trinity International University every summer. I haven't decided if I will complete my master's.

In May 2011, I took training in conflict coaching and mediation from Peacemakers Ministry. I have found that what I learned helps me almost every day. Our lives are filled with conflict; we can't avoid it. It's helpful to have a healthy way to deal with it. I have also had opportunities to use this training by teaching a course in church and applying the principles in a ministry that I am involved in.

I was asked to become a member of the board of directors of a ministry for homeless mothers in Sparta called Sojourners Journey. I am very active in this ministry. As I mentioned earlier, I participated in a general surgery mission trip to Honduras in March 2012. That was a great experience. My husband and I have hosted "The Truth Project" and hope to do another session soon.

I have had the opportunity to be a patient advocate for one person and hope to do more of that. I have offered my services as a medical professional in our area. We live about thirty minutes from the nearest ambulance service. I asked about becoming a first responder, but you have to be a firefighter in order to do that here, and I don't think I want to do that. I have let the 911 personnel know I am here, and they have my phone number.

Last year I was asked to be the backup medical director for the Tomah Memorial Hospital Hospice program. It requires me to keep up my license, which means I have to get continuing medical education credits. I enjoy going to conferences and learning. I like being part of the hospice program. I think it is an excellent program. I only have to work if the medical director is unavailable, and I relieve him for a weekend once a quarter.

I feel that I am part of a community for the first time in my life. I never had the time to get to know my neighbors before. I remember reading a book once on how I could become more organized so I would have time to have tea with friends. I realized I was more organized than what they were proposing in the book and that I still didn't have the time. So now I am taking advantage of having the time to spend with friends, neighbors, and family. We have tea together.

I am also a member of the Cranberry Homemakers. They made a donation to help me publish this book.

It sounds as if I am very busy, but I'm doing things I want to do when I want to do them. My time is my own. That makes a big difference. I like to be busy. Now that I am finishing this book, I will have time to do something else. I believe lots of opportunities are out there if you are willing to try new things. My approach is I do what God has for me to do each day—and I look forward to what God has for me in the future.

CPSIA information can be obtained
at www.ICGtesting.com
Printed in the USA
FFOW05n1617020215